BABY

187 things we've learned

BOOMERS

that you need to know NOW...

SPEAK!

whatever your age!

RIX QUINN

ISBN: 1-4196-8303-9
ISBN-13: 9781419683039

Visit www.booksurge.com to order additional copies.

Dedication

To Erica, my beloved and wise wife, a joy to be around.

To Katie, a loving and brilliant daughter, who lights my world every day.

To Dad Bill and Mom Lennie, who taught me that there is beauty and potential in everyone.

Table of Contents

Foreword   7

About the Author   9

Introduction   11

1 -- How we conducted this Baby Boomer survey   13

2 -- Seven things a bunch of us share   17

3 – Are Baby Boomers "Average Americans"?   29

4 – How did Boomer kids spend an average day?   33

5 – A typical household in middle-class
    Boomertown   45

6 – What happened in elementary school?   55

7 – How we rated grades…and teachers   59

8 – Favorite games and toys for girls and boys   65

9 – How to get by in junior high   73

10 – Did you have these thoughts in high school? 77

11 – Rags, wheels, and other teen trends   81

12 – Boomers talk about their best friends   87

13 – Our favorite books…or, tome-sweet-tome   93

14 – Why Boomers squeeze time: the
    compression factor   97

15 – Movie favorites: just pop culture, or our
    generation's true beliefs?   101

16 – Best years of TV for you and me   107

17 – Most memorable day of a Boomer's life?   121

18 – Who had the greatest influence on us?   127

19 – Comments and compliments that made big
     impressions   131

20 – The question people asked most: "What
     do you want to be when you grow up?"   137

21 – Over 50,000 people Baby Boomers admire   143

22 – What famous people would you like
     to meet, or invite to dinner?   151

23 – How should we prepare to face the future? 157

24 – What have you done that makes you proud? 163

25 – Ten school lessons we never forgot   167

26 – What the heck happened to Main Street?   169

27 -- Going back, looking forward: Nine tips
     for a memorable class reunion   175

28 – The final chapter: Should you write
     your own obituary?   179

29 – Epilogue   183

30 – Bonus: 25 startling predictions for
     Boomers and their children   185

Foreword

Our high school class gathers for a reunion at least once every five years. There were a bunch of us – over 1000 originally – but over time we've lost track of several, and a few have passed away.

At the last reunion, I stood in a long line waiting to get my name tag. I struck up a conversation with the guy behind me, a man I swear I'd never seen before. He asked who I ran with, I asked about his friends, and we realized we had no acquaintances in common.

We were complete strangers, but we'd spent three years at the same high school, shared the same lunchroom and hallways…and that's about all. We finally reached the name tag table, picked up our badges, then headed off in opposite directions, strangers again.

Connect and disconnect

On a larger scale, this seems to be common to our generation. Prior generations, like our parents' Greatest Generation or Silent Generation, shared a large number of beliefs.

Ours, in contrast, has often been divided. First, by young men's desire to grow their hair longer, or keep it short. Then by the Vietnam War. Then by education. Then by political alliances.

In short…we've stayed apart too long. This book is an effort to reunite us. To help us focus not on our differences, but on our similarities.

For whatever time is left to us (hopefully 30 years or

more), we could unite to change society for the better. With our time, training, and monetary resources, we could make a great gift to this world.

After reading this, we hope you'll agree that together we've shared so much history, we should reconnect to shape the future. — *Rix Quinn*

About the Author

Rix Quinn lives in Fort Worth, Texas. He attended public schools there, and graduated from Paschal High School. An early Baby Boomer (born prior to 1955), he experienced much of the history discussed by other Boomers in this book.

He holds a B.A. degree in journalism from Texas Christian University, and a M.A. from California State University.

He went to work for his father's business magazine publishing company in the late 1970's, and during 20-plus years served as a magazine editor and publisher.

After the company sold its magazines, he began to produce short features for both network radio and newspapers.

Today he writes two weekly columns – one on Baby Boomers – for the national newspaper syndicate DBR Media. He also conducts writing workshops for colleges, education service centers, and area school districts.

Rix has written three books: Words That Stick: A Guide to Short Writing with Big Impact (Ten Speed Press); Superpowers: Building Human Skills for Superhuman Performance (Amazon Shorts); and How News Stories Can Help You Solve Problems (Amazon Shorts).

Introduction

Have you looked at your birth certificate lately? If it says you were born between 1946 and 1964, welcome to my world. You and I are officially considered "Baby Boomers."

What do we have in common? Well, we're over 40, but not yet over the hill. Sadly, a few of our unfortunate members are under a hill somewhere, taking the eternal dirt nap.

But the rest of us share a unique time and space. We were born in the middle of the 20th century, and hope to live to the middle of the 21st. When our earliest members were born, only 141 million people lived in the U.S. Today there are over 303 million.

And we Boomers make up over 78 million – or about 26 percent – of Americans. That means we're vitally important to the media who want to reach us, to the nation's retailers, to our growing children, and to our aging parents.

And, in a few years, we'll be major consumers of all those geriatric products we're only beginning to stock now.

Think about what we've witnessed in the last 40-60 years. We've seen television grow into an enormously influential medium. We've observed a space program that took humans to the moon, and returned them safely to the earth.

Where are we going as we age? Will we someday be viewed by our children and grandchildren as a great generation? Will we make this world a better place?

One of my friends died prematurely, in his 40's. But not long before he passed away, he told me one thing really bothered him.

"I haven't done all I wanted to do," he said. "I wonder — if somebody cares to judge my walk across four decades — if they'll discover that I left any footprints."

What sort of footprints will you leave for others to follow?

CHAPTER 1
How we conducted this Baby Boomer survey

We've always wondered what answers we'd get from contemporaries if we gave them complete anonymity to discuss their Boomer childhoods. So, over a few months we compiled a list of questions designed to find out what they had learned over four or more exciting decades.

Please consider me a "humorous historian," one who looks at the past, marvels at some of the weird things that happened, then tries to see the lighter side of it. Now, on to the research:

- The focus group – those receiving questionnaires – consisted of men and women born between the years of 1946 and 1964, the time span generally referred to as the "Baby Boomer Generation."
- Because this writer has been termed "mathematically challenged," no attempt was made to draw a statistically accurate sample. (That has been done by several others, probably better than we could attempt to do.)
- This is an attitudinal survey, NOT a statistical one. No attempt was made to catalog people by gender, race, education, or other categories. (These surveys and statistics already exist.)
- The questioner tried – in every way possible – to avoid addressing gender, racial, religious,

political, topical, or any other controversial issues.

- Over the course of a two-month span, approximately 50 people were asked to participate in this focus group. Some people in the original group suggested others for participation. These people were also sent questionnaires.

Baby Boomers born between 1946 and 1954 are often called Early Boomers. Those born between 1955 and 1964 are sometimes called Generation Jones to distinguish them from older Boomers and Generation X, which immediately followed them.

- Some people chose to answer all questions. Some people answered only a few of the questions. Some who were originally sent questionnaires elected not to participate.
- Those originally asked to participate were acquaintances the writer had met in social or business settings. The group is fairly geographically diverse, and is fairly evenly divided between females and males.

- The focus group is sub-divided into two groups: "older Boomers" born from 1946 to 1954, and "younger Boomers" born between 1955 and 1964. Many studies have been made separating these two groups who were subjected to different social issues. (Example: Older male Boomers faced the potential of a military draft; younger male Boomers did not.)

- Because Boomers are probably history's most statistically-analyzed generation, we sought to take a different path. We primarily looked for three things: (1) How did Boomers interpret events from their history? (2) How did Boomers interact with their own social group, and with mentors, the generation before them, and the generation which followed? (3) How do Boomers perceive their generation's impact on society?

- To protect privacy, no names were used in this study. First and last initials assigned to various replies were changed to protect anonymity.

- Many of the survey questions asked participants to recall specific events. We looked for memorable national and personal events that shaped the adults Boomers became.

- The writer spent about 20 years in the magazine field, and has had some experience creating attitudinal questionnaires. These particular questionnaires ask open-ended questions, those requiring more than a yes-or-no reply.

- IMPORTANT! This book contains some exaggerations and punch lines in an effort to be "funny." These are intentional. However, the quotes from Boomers are real.

CHAPTER 2
Seven things a bunch of us share

Are you a Baby Boomer? Is your parent? Do you know what a Baby Boomer is?

In the U.S. alone, there are about 78 million of us. Every forth person you see at the dentist, carwash, or leg waxing salon is a Boomer. This means that (1) we still have some of our own teeth, (2) we may drive around aimlessly, and (3) some of us grow hair where we don't want it.

Boomers lived through both good times (man on the moon) and bad (mooning cars). We survived the gas shortage of 1978, and now manufacture our own intestinally. We survived the Cold War, and now endure frequent colds.

What shapes a Boomer's thinking? Can all Baby Boomers still think? Do you really care?

You really should care. Because – unless we run out of retro music – one or more of us will run the world for the next 25 years.

Understanding us

Here's a personal story. It's the early 1960's, and we're sitting in elementary school. Around 10 AM, the school bell suddenly blasts three-and-a-half times.

Three rings means a tornado, and four signals an air raid. (Definition of "air raid": A nuclear attack followed by desperation, radiation, and vaporization.)

Because we're not sure if we heard three or four rings, we don't know what to do. In a tornado, we're taught to open windows and doors. If it's an air raid, we're supposed to close them.

So, we stumble over each other into the school hall way. If it's a tornado, we're supposed to sit against the lockers.

If it's an air raid, we put our heads between our knees, and cover our scalps with our hands. (This technique was known as "duck and cover." How it protects from nuclear explosion is a mystery to me.)

Somebody asks, "Is this a tornado or an air raid?" But the teacher doesn't know, so we just kill time until the principal tells us it's a false alarm.

And that's what we've been doing these last four decades...killing time between personal storms and false alarms.

We're still not sure if the next news event is simply hot wind or glowing, radioactive cinders. But after surviving this long, we figure that the only thing we have to fear is fear itself. (Well, fear and TV reality shows.)

Lesson # 1: We're pessimists by nature, but we bounce back quickly from defeat because we expect it.

Davy Crockett, Annie Oakley, and Superman

No, these three are not some 60's folk group. These people – actually two people and a Kryptonian – became major heroes to the Boomer generation.

Davy Crockett was a fabled American frontiersman, Congressman, and defender of the Alamo. Boomers remember him as the guy who made a series of movies with his sidekick Georgie Russell, who later became Jedd Clampett in the "Beverly Hillbillies."

The television Davy Crockett appealed to Boomer boys for five reasons:

1. He spent a lot of time riding and fighting, and very little time talking to girls.
2. Lots of people hung around him, did everything he said, and told him what an awesome adventurer he was.
3. He wore a fringed shirt, buckskin pants, and moccasins, setting a fashion trend that flourished in the 1960's.
4. After he got killed (or at least injured pretty seriously) at the Alamo, he returned to star in two sequels.
5. He could sing, dance, play the guitar, and write original music. Obviously, getting caught at the Alamo was a bad career move.

Next, let's look at Annie Oakley. Not the real one who toured with Buffalo Bill's Wild West Show, but the TV Annie with that form-fitting leather skirt.

The television Oakley appealed to Boomer girls for five reasons:

1. If a guy gave her trouble, she simply shot him. Women who do this today face up to three months' jail time.

2   She had a boyfriend/sidekick named Lofty, who agreed with everything she said. (My wife would term this a "reasonable male.")

3. She could run, fight, or shoot, yet her hair never got out of place.

4. She had a kid brother named Tag she could also boss around. And like Lofty, Tag never talked back because...hey, she's Annie Oakley.

5. She didn't appear to work, but she always had plenty of money.

Finally, let's examine Superman. He's a guy who attracts both genders because:

1. He can fly. How cool is that?

2. He's really good-looking and gentlemanly, and how many guys can get away with a cape?

3. He's immune to human disease, pain, and suffering (like many politicians). The only thing that affects him is Kryptonite, which is scarcer than Hillary campaign stickers at a Republican primary.

4. He's surrounded by dummies. He puts on his glasses, he's Clark Kent. He yanks them off, he's Superman. But nobody in Metropolis can figure this out. Duh!

5. And don't forget he can fly. Far. And fast. And upside down, if he wants to.

These are the heroes who shaped our childhoods. We modeled our behavior from theirs. (And a few of us actually tried to fly. These deceased individuals are called the Fall-Down-Go Boomers.)

So, whenever you find a Boomer in a tough situation today, expect that person to sing, dance, saddle a horse, or put on a cape.

Lesson # 2: We believe that if given half a chance, we can achieve great things.

A Day of Boomer Childhood

To comprehend the adult, you must first know the child. (Some guy said this at my "fulfillment" workshop. I'm pretty sure it means that when we grow up we stay the same, except we buy bigger underwear.)

A Boomer's elementary school day started early, when he sat down for breakfast with the family. Back then, mid-century kids ate food cooked on a stove, or right out of a cereal box that contained a prize. The "microwave" was a small hand gesture used to greet neighbors you didn't know.

Unless you lived far from school (50 miles or more), you walked or rode a bike. Sometimes one kid pedaled the bike, and another kid sat on the metal book rack behind the seat. This explains why some of us could not reproduce.

The school day contained six hours of classroom work interrupted by two recess periods plus a lunch. Many younger kids opted for the "plate lunch" (one meat and two certified vegetables) plus a small carton of white or chocolate milk.

There was one teacher-supervised recess where children played kickball, volleyball, or any activity with an inflated round object. Unsupervised recess allowed "free play," but those who played too freely – with car radiators, schoolyard animals, or that whip brought to "show and tell" – won a trip to the principal's office.

Lesson # 3: Independent by nature, we are still traditionalists by nurture. We have positive motives, but ask that you leave us alone to solve problems.

Additional Education

The average Boomer spent at least 12 years in school. Over 20% spent over 16 years. A few Boomers are still going to school. If they time things right, they'll collect a diploma and Social Security simultaneously.

Some researchers – many of them also Boomers – brag that we're the most educated generation in history. Why?

1. We are the children of Depression-era parents who stressed education as a door-opener to higher paying jobs and a more affluent life.
2. Many of us grew up during a time this country used a "military draft," which meant that males 18 and over could be called into military service.
3. Many of us also came of age during the Vietnam conflict, when military service could mean an all-expenses paid trip to a war zone.
4. Many of us could delay military conscription by requesting the popular "2-S" deferment, which

meant we were full-time students.

5. A few of us found we could maintain a student status after college graduation by attending graduate school.

6. Stepping into another classroom was infinitely safer than stepping into combat.

7. Therefore, many Boomers now hold more degrees than a meat thermometer.

Lesson # 4: We are the most educated generation in history. We believe in learning and new technologies, and pass those lessons on to our children.

A brief look at the 1950s

It's not fair to ask Boomers about the 1950's, because many of us weren't born. Most of us remember parts of the 1960's and 1970's, even though some of us were either very young or very stoned.

If you didn't experience these important decades, we'll share the big events with you. And if you were there – but for some reason don't remember – we'll refresh you.

Think of the 1950's as an episode of "Leave in to Beaver" or "Father Knows Best." It was a time of tranquility, a time for sharing family values. Also, most of it was in black-and-white.

Nearly everybody wore some sort of suit to identify his profession. Business people wore coats and ties. Tennis pros wore white shirts and shorts. Crazy people wore straightjackets, and rarely ran for public office.

During this decade, the Baby Boom grew exponentially. Young adults moved to the suburbs when homebuilders completed huge housing developments. Once settled into new homes, couples started families because (1) they wanted several children and (2) there were few late-night talk shows to delay procreation.

Because there were so many of us, states quickly constructed schools to contain us. Educators also developed scholarly "film strips" to help instructors explain complicated concepts.

Film strips were like slide shows. Each was accompanied by audio. The teacher moved to the next slide every time the audio "beeped." (One time this kid in our class made random beep sounds. The teacher raced through the slides, leaving us several minutes of mind-numbing audio about hibernating snakes.)

Did you ever see a film strip? Did anybody in your class die from boredom? My two favorite film strips were "From caterpillar to butterfly" and "Mr. Gorilla learns to drive." (Actually I made that last one up, because I never saw a film strip about a gorilla driver, especially one who could pass the written exam.)

Lesson # 5: We are the first generation to be educated visually via TV, movies, and now computers. We first must see something to comprehend it, and expect reinforcement from both audio messages and others' feedback.

Welcome to the 1960's

The first part of the decade brought this country a new, young President, John F. Kennedy. The end of the decade ushered in hippies, drugs, and free love.

The questions you should probably ask are: (1) What happened to the middle of the decade? (2) What are hippies? (3) How much did love cost before it was free?

(1) Most of us don't remember what happened during those middle years because we hit puberty. It's long been suspected that a person cannot hit puberty and retain useful information simultaneously.

(2) Hippies were children of the 60's who focused on love, peace, and music. A few also focused on recreational drugs, which they used until their eyes unfocused. They wore outrageous clothing, headbands and long hair. Many also removed their bras (some of these were female).

But seriously, illicit drugs played a big role in the decade. Take LSD, for instance (and many did).

This potent hallucinogen was also called "acid." The substance caused users to "trip out." Sadly, a few of them took a permanent trip to the hereafter, and are now taking the "dirt nap" we mentioned earlier.

Lesson # 6: Much conservative thought today has been seeded by our fear that we might repeat liberal missteps of 40 years ago. However, history reminds us that progressive thought to correct social injustice is what made the country grow.

A glance at the 1970's

Boomers who did not grow up in the 1960's grew up in the 1970's. At least they became adults. A few, of course, never grew up. In 30 years, you will see them in retirement homes overdosing on laxatives and staging walker races to the toilet.

The 1970's are remembered for unique fads like leisure suits and streaking.

Leisure suits (shirt-like jacket and matching slack) dominated men's wear. Guys hoped this fashion – which didn't require a tie – would replace business suits. Those men who chose leisure suits gave away all their ties, and today may be banned from financial meetings (but rarely sales conferences).

Leisure suits came in bright fluorescent shades, colors not found in nature. However, men could generally find an open-collar shirt to match those suits. You'll see many of these outrageous outfits at garage sales today, often priced at "Make me any offer."

To understand streaking, one must first understand that the 1970's reinvented male nudeness. Before this decade, men appeared naked only in locker rooms and physical exams.

But during the 1970's, nakedness became fashionable in dramatic presentations. Many men – and women – thus assumed that public nakedness was acceptable in short bursts, especially if everybody else was wearing a leisure suit.

"Streakers" were men and women who removed all their clothes and sprinted through public areas dressed in birthday suits, even though it was not their birthday.

To hide their identities, several wore masks. This made absolutely no sense, because nobody looked at their faces.

Lesson # 7: As a group, we tend to be image conscious. We are willing to spend large amounts of money for discretionary purchases if marketers can give us a reason to rationalize the purchase.

Chapter 3
Are Baby Boomers average Americans?

If you grew up somewhere in the neighborhood of 1955–1975, you probably considered yourself an "average American." Sadly, we don't hear that term today...which may be a reflection on the impact we've made on society. How?

This "average American" researched back to 1955. I viewed both written surveys and training films from that time. Here's what I learned:

1. Nearly 40% of the U.S. population had a family income of $3-$6,000.
2. Another 30% had an income of $6–$10,000. That's an astounding 70% of Americans who saw themselves in the middle to upper-middle class category.
3. Upper income folks – those who earned over $10,000 a year – were applauded as those business owners or leaders who created new opportunities for the others.
4. Another impressive statistic: about 85% of the total national income went to 93% of families... an equitable distribution of wealth.

What? Are these statistics making you sleepy? Well, wake up and keep reading, because the prose gets better now.

Without boring you with more statistics, it appears that no matter where we Boomers fell on the income scale, the vast percentage of us considered ourselves to be "middle class." And in the 1950's and 1960's, we were probably right.

What does this mean?

If we considered ourselves to be middle class, let me make two assumptions: (1) we felt relatively secure, and could concentrate on other things rather than mere survival, and (2) we assumed that if we got an education (including college training) and worked hard, we could secure an even better future.

What's more, most of our role models said they came from middle class or modest backgrounds. For example:

a. America's President during the 1950's, Dwight Eisenhower, came from a large family of modest means in Abilene, Kansas.

b. His Vice-President, Richard Nixon, was the son of a California grocer.

c. Most of America's first astronauts were young military pilots who had received college educations.

d. Most of baseball's and football's professional heroes claimed to come from working class families.

e. Virtually all the situation comedies of the 1950's and 1960's depicted middle class families. (Examples: Father Knows Best, Leave It to

Beaver, The Andy Griffith Show, Dobie Gillis, The Dick Van Dyke Show.)

The notable exception to this was wealthy John F. Kennedy, the Democratic President elected in 1960 who championed civil rights, the Peace Corps, and other initiatives benefiting less-fortunate people. And he used his power and position to improve the lives of struggling Americans.

What did we learn?

1. We came of age in simpler and more hopeful times. Yes, we faced atomic threats, but most were short-lived and vague.

2. Our generation's own children – who range in age from teens to early 30's – have grown up in a far more dangerous time, and have witnessed huge disparity politically. They've witnessed horrible terrorist acts, and have ridden an economic roller coaster in recent years.

3. Traditional manufacturing and distribution jobs have been "outsourced" to other countries in order to save a few dollars. But at what eventual cost?

4. And, back in our days (that sounds old, doesn't it?), the Congressional and executive branches seemed to work more closely together.

5. Finally, you don't hear folks talk much today about how much fun it is to be "middle class."

Why? Maybe we just don't feel middle class – or united – any more.

CHAPTER 4
Boomer kids tell us about an 'average day'

Three things Baby Boomer childhoods shared: (1) feelings of freedom, (2) constant outdoor activities, and (3) bicycles.

"We roamed the neighborhood at will," laughed D.L. "That was a significant area, typically limited only by four-lane roads. Alleys, culverts, trails, and creeks were all part of this urban territory.

"Our parents knew where we were, and were aware of the usual suspects with us. Bikes – BMX motocross style – were the transportation of choice.

"We typically participated in three activities: (1) sports, almost entirely football and baseball, with football being primary; (2) biking, bike customization, stunts, jumps, racing, hide-and-seek, and knocking over trash cans; and (3) playing army, picking sides, making forts, searching-and-destroying, camouflage, and other war games.

"What did we fear? Dogs, tree limbs breaking, skinned knees, and bike wrecks."

Pre-school

"I remember days in the car," said J.L. "Very relaxed. No car seats. No seat belts.

"Normally, I would stand in the middle of the front seat...no console either. I stood there until I was too tall and had to bend over to see out the front window.

"One time my Mom and I were taking my grandmother out to my aunt's farm when I spotted what looked like this huge mushroom cloud. Remember those Cold War days?

"It turned out to be an explosion from a fireworks stand just outside of town.

"Also, my Dad would often let me 'drive' on the country roads. I would sit on his lap and steer, and we'd sing 'The Eyes of Texas' really loud. I thought that was the state song until I was in high school."

School days

"Almost every day," J.J. remembered, "I'd walk home from school carrying a heavy load of books. We'd stop and get a Coke float at the shopping center's drug store, or we'd get a hamburger at a family-owned restaurant also in the center."

"During the school year my brothers and I got up, made our beds, ate breakfast, and walked to school with friends. I love reading, spelling, and social studies," R.R. recollected.

"We usually stopped on the way home at a little convenience store that had cold drinks that were iced down in a big red Coca-Cola container in front of the store. We bought candy lipstick and candy cigarettes, and walked the rest of the way home.

"We watched cartoons or American Bandstand on alternating nights. I helped Mom either set the table, cook dinner, or clean off the table to do dishes."

GOODBYE, DICK AND JANE

Say...do you remember first grade? I do...I spent a wonderful year there, and nearly got asked to stay longer.

The best part of the day? When we read those wonderful stories about Dick and Jane.

If you grew up in the 1950's or 1960's, you probably remember them, too. They were those two nice kids who lived in a nice house on a nice street somewhere in America.

They had a dog named Spot, and a cat named Puff...and I think they had a little brother or sister, too.

Anyway, one of the people who wrote the Dick and Jane primers died in 1998, and I thought you'd like to know. His name was Sterl Artley, and he was a famous reading teacher.

His simple stories began with basic words, gradually building children's vocabulary and word recognition skills. Unfortunately, it's hard to find Dick and Jane books anymore. Many educators chose to move on to different methods.

I'll always remember Dick and Jane fondly, because they taught me to read. And they also taught me to keep building my vocabulary, to keep growing, and to treat my doggy and kitty friends well too.

See Rix cry. Dick and Jane sad too. No more adventures. But many, many Baby Boomer friends.

Can you say Baby Boomers getting older? Too bad, too bad. Goodbye, Dick and Jane. Goodbye, childhood. Hello, Arthur Ritus.

School food

"In elementary school I remember how delicious that cafeteria food was because it was real home cooking done on-site," recalled G.M. "The only food I didn't like was hash. But we had home fried chicken and catfish, as well as good barbeque and fresh vegetables.

One older Boomer said he remembers that lunch at his elementary school "cost 37 cents. That included one meat, two vegetables, a fluffy roll, and a choice of milk or a flavored orange drink."

"Also, we paid a dime on a few Fridays and got to experience some culture. Entertainers on the Southern School Assembly circuit presented magic shows, singing, playing instruments, and telling stories. One of them was a professional whistler who did the whistling for the old radio show 'The Whistler.'"

Neighborhood activities

"We had neighborhood pick-up ball games most afternoons," recalled L.R. "Although they may have existed in previous generations, we had more leisure time. Now, all children's sports are organized."

"The red-haired lady who lived at the end of our block was single," another Boomer remembered, "and the first person to build a fence around her back yard. She sun-bathed, and got caught drinking beer once. There weren't any kids around at the time, but once was enough to give her a 'wild woman' reputation.

"She would pull her TV out to the front door and set up lawn chairs in her front yard. All the neighborhood kids would sit out there, and we'd watch Your Show of Shows, Lawrence Welk, Mitch Miller, The Gary Moore Show, Jack Benny, Burns & Allen, and others.

"All shows were that lady's choice, of course, but we all thought she was really cool."

Remembered T.C.: "Many kids gathered at a house up the street — I don't think I ever knew anyone in the family — where there was a trampoline in the driveway...on the concrete, no net! The general feeling was apparently of safety and neighborliness, not fearfulness."

Halloween

Most Boomers remember some wild Halloween stories. But here's one with a slightly different twist:

"I remember when Halloween died," said A.T. "I was in the 7th grade in 1975, and had dressed up as Quasimodo to go trick-or-treating with my best friend in her neighborhood directly west of a golf course.

"This was during the time of the urban legend of razor blades and hypodermic needles in candy. When we got back to her house to review our haul, we each found several pieces of bubble gum pre-chewed by some thoughtful goblin and then painstakingly rewrapped.

"That was the last time I went trick-or-treating."

Summertime

"In the summer," said R.H., "my friends and I would play a lot of football or baseball. And we loved to play cowboys, or 'Combat.'"

"We were out of the house right after breakfast, while it was still cool," a lady Boomer remembered. "We terrorized the neighborhood on our bikes that were all souped up with baseball cards attached to the spokes of the wheels with clothespins. My bike was blue with fancy handlebars that had plastic fringe coming out of the handgrips!

"We climbed trees and skated the sidewalks with clip-on skates, and no summer was complete without thoroughly skinned knees and elbows. Mom gave me pocket change to walk up to a nearby food store to buy milk, bread, or cold drinks. I always had my little brothers in tow, and we held hands and flew across the busy street when it was safe to cross."

A couple of Boomers also remembered summer vacation car trips. "Every day we'd wake up really early, and drive as far as we could before dark," one said. "We kids had only one request: stop at a motel where there's a swimming pool."

Lessons

"After-school lessons," emphasized K.L. "Everyone I knew was signed up for lessons...piano, art, dance, etiquette. I don't think our parents were subjected to endless lessons."

"Somewhere around 6th grade," a male Boomer recalled, "some kid – or a kid's mom – got information on ballroom dance lessons being offered by two or three different studios. Suddenly this became a trendy thing. Every person wanted to take lessons at the same studio as his friends.

"As I remember, kids signed up for a series of 12 to 15 lessons, one each week. After that, a bunch of the kids signed up for another series.

"This went on for two years. All I remember is that dancing conflicted with baseball."

Room to roam

"I grew up in a neighborhood that was located above the city zoo and surrounding park area," P.M. said. "In the summer the whole neighborhood of kids got on bicycles and rode to the zoo, unsupervised. We took our sack lunches, bought a drink, looked at the animals, and then played baseball on the diamonds in the park.

"We weren't afraid of being out by ourselves, and we had the best summers ever."

Said D.W.: "I walked home from school after basketball practice – about two miles – unaccompanied. I walked into my parents' front door, which was unlocked. We kids stayed outside late into the night, parents didn't worry about what might befall us, or what we might get into."

Bikes and more bikes

"I loved my bicycle," C. T. said. "The bike itself wasn't anything special, probably a hand-me-down from my sister, but it represented total freedom. I could roam the neighborhood all summer long, as long as I was back by dinner, escaping again afterwards only to return by dark.

"My friends and I would meet on the playground of an elementary school around the corner of my house, or I'd ride up to the shopping center to blow my miniscule allowance on candy at the drug store."

"I could ride the bike to school, and travel blocks from home without fear," J.H. said.

"One day I fell off my bike while running an errand for Mother," L.H. remarked. "When I got home, with bright green grass stains on my brand new white shirt, Mom already knew I'd had a wreck because someone in the neighborhood notified her immediately.

"What I think is unique about that is: she was thankful the woman let her know. Today's mom would probably consider that 'none of the woman's business,' and that if her son fell off the bike at high speed he had some special purpose in doing so."

"There was no concern about dangerous strangers," D.S. agreed. "Dad went to work, and Mom sent us outside to play all day with little supervision. I rode my bike around the neighborhood both day and evening. Neither I nor my parents were concerned about my safety."

The drivers' license

"I'll always remember the day I received my unrestricted driver's license," noted F.T. "As I recall, that was age 16.

"Boomers have a love affair with cars, and the automotive age truly underwent a 'power shift' with people born from 1946–1964."

Tornado and 'air raid' drills

"I grew up in the region called 'Tornado Alley,'" one older Boomer noted. "This meant we practiced tornado drills – leaving the school room and going into the hall – all the time.

"And, since this was the Cold War period, we also practiced 'air raid drills.' They were like tornado drills, but more complicated.

"Anyway, some friends and I remember air raid drills where our moms were instructed to come to the school, and line up their cars. When the emergency bell rang, we were supposed to file out of the school, and hop into cars. The first five kids got in the first car, the next five in the second, and so on.

"In an actually emergency, I guess the cars were supposed to take us somewhere."

"What was unrealistic about that," J.D. added, "was that you were supposed to get in the first car available, whether it was your mom's or not. My mother would have raised Cain until she found me, then she'd load everybody else in."

"I remember a Civil Defense shelter sign on our building," she added, "but I never knew what it meant or that it actually led anywhere."

Emotional extremes

It's a thousand wonders," comments R.R. "that our generation isn't any more messed up than we are. Our constant, conflicting partners in life were going out to play with our buddies without a care in the world, and the threat of imminent annihilation!"

What did we learn?

1. Our early years were neighborhood-oriented. Our schools, friends, stores, and play areas were generally within walking distance.

2. Few safety features existed. There were no car seat belts or children's car seats. We received few comments on toy restrictions or fear of dangerous playthings.

3. Outdoor activities dominated after-school activities. Most respondents told us that both they and their parents felt comfortable with their children

having free access to the neighborhood. Without fence laws, neighborhood pets enjoyed roaming, too.

4. Walking or bike-riding were the two primary means of transportation. Strip shopping centers – generally containing a grocery, barber, ladies hair solon, pharmacy with a breakfast/luncheon counter ("drug store"), hardware store, bike shop, "five-and-dime" store, and neighborhood hamburger restaurant ("malt shop") were prevalent across America. Neighborhoods were self-contained, and provided most primary needs.

5. Respondents complimented school food, which many said was made fresh daily at the school.

6. Frequent school assemblies introduced Boomers to useful skills like home and fire safety, music, art, history, and information about prevailing 1950's and 1960's American culture and values.

7. After-school activities are generally remembered as free, fun, and unstructured, a far different situation from the 21st century's highly organized, timed, controlled children's environments.

8. Conversely, a large number of Boomers told us they took piano, dance, guitar, horn, or other type of lesson on a regular basis. Apparently it benefited them, because many have suggested that their children take lessons, too.

9. The bicycle symbolized freedom and access to Boomers. It's perhaps the most valued and used possession of a Boomer's childhood.

10. The driver's license represented a major milestone. Automakers also benefited from the huge number of Boomers who bought new and used cars

in great numbers, and at younger ages than prior generations.

11. The Cold War – and ongoing threat of atomic attack – hung above Boomers' heads. Many spoke of non-specific but very real fears about potential threats.

12. Most respondents spoke positively about their early childhoods.

CHAPTER 5
A typical household in middle-class Boomertown

If you are a Boomer, you'll recognize nearly everything we talk about in this chapter. If you're not, get ready to climb aboard a time machine that whisks you back into recent history.

Most of this stuff pertains to both the 1950's and 1960's. Since Boomers came from all ethnicities and all economic sectors, we may have experienced these things at different times.

For instance, I interviewed some Boomers who said they clearly recall when the first BLACK-AND-WHITE television appeared in their neighborhoods. (I do not.)

Good morning

Welcome back to the mid-1950's. Our anonymous boy (let's give him the nickname "Boomer," OK?) is an elementary school student in a mid-sized town in the middle of America. Where? It doesn't really matter.

Boomer's alarm clock – non-electric, something he probably wound the night before – goes off at 7 AM. It's a nice day in early fall. School started the day after Labor Day for him, and just about every other kid around the country.

Extra trivia: Many boys knew when school began because on Labor Day the college all-stars from the previous year played the National Football League pro champs. (This was before the Super Bowl, which began in 1967.)

Boomer's nearsighted, so he reaches for his glasses next to his twin bed. (Contact lenses weren't available yet.) Since it's warm outside, he goes to the window and turns off his window fan. (Some homes now have window air conditioning units...awesome!)

Next, he goes to the front door to see what fresh treats the milkman left. The milkman – if you didn't have one – is a guy who brought products like milk, cream, ice cream, and butter right to the front door every morning. (You could tell him what you wanted by leaving one of your empty glass milk bottles on the porch the night before.)

What's for breakfast? If Mom's busy in the kitchen, it could be scrambled eggs, bacon, sausage, hash brown potatoes, toast, maybe even biscuits and gravy. No worries about cholesterol then. What was cholesterol?

Boomer's little sister and brother are already up, and also getting ready for school. Dad has probably already left for work.

Mom gives the kids lunch money (25 to 50 cents each), makes sure they've got their books, then takes them out to the front yard in time for the school bus to pick them up. The family's got one car, and Dad takes it to work.

Once the kids get off to school, Mom hand-washes the breakfast dishes (no dishwashers), then washes clothes. When she's done with the clothes, she takes them outside to dry on a clothesline…which works great, if it doesn't rain. (Sounds like ancient times, doesn't it?)

Next, Mom started planning the evening meal. Short of time? Well, she could buy one of those new "TV dinners" that came frozen, and cook it in the oven. (This is the pre-microwave era.)

SERVICE STATIONS

Whenever we needed gasoline or car repair, my Dad and I would head for the neighborhood "full service" station. The uniformed attendants would come out to take gasoline requests, then provide all sorts of extra services while the tank filled. They'd wash your windows, check your oil levels, and check your tire pressure.

Later, when I got my own car, I drove right to the same place. I was just a kid, but they treated me like a king.

"Check the tires?" the attendant would ask as he filled the tank, followed by "How's the family?" or "How's your Dad's car running?"

I was just there for fuel. But if the engine knocked, a tire felt low, or a belt came off, I'd come back there in an instant. What happened to that wonderful place?

At school

Boomer's school is convenient, right in his neighborhood. The day begins with the principal's announcements, followed by the Pledge of Allegiance, followed by a prayer. (Separation of church and state? Huh?)

Next come grade-appropriate school courses, maybe a recess, and pretty soon it's time for LUNCH!

Kids can bring their lunch in a sack or lunchbox from home. Many do that, and the lunchbox often contains at thermal drink bottle, too.

At the first of school, we always wanted to see our friends' new lunch boxes. Most carried the faces of TV action heroes or cartoon characters. Today – if you'd held onto those old boxes – they might fetch you some good money from collectors.

But I haven't talked to a single friend who kept his. I quit taking mine to work when I turned 31.

Boomer's mom gave him lunch money, so he goes through the line and selects a meat, two vegetables, a roll, a dessert, and a drink for an economical price.

After lunch, the teacher reads her students a story while many half-listen and half-doze. Next come afternoon classes, and around 3:30 the school day ends.

After school

As discussed earlier, kids generally came to school one of four ways: they walked, rode their bikes, took the bus, or rode in a carpool with neighbors. After school, Boomer's friends invite him to walk home, and get a snack on the way.

Now, this is before the fast food days. Boomer's friends can stop by the pharmacy (called the "drug store" then), where they can get soft drinks or desserts from the "soda fountain." Or, there's a family-owned burger stand nearby, a place where lots of cool kids hang out to play the jukebox…a record player than holds loads of music.

After that, Boomer and his buddies head home to watch afternoon children's shows. They love the Mickey Mouse Club, which showcases talented kids their own age.

And speaking of talent, once a week a music teacher comes to Boomer's house to teach him and his sister how to play piano. Boomer's sister is good. Boomer is incredibly lousy. Maybe his mom will sign him up to try a different instrument next year.

Sports, sports, sports

Boomers grew up in a sports-hungry society. We youngsters spent a good part of our weekends watching college, Olympic, or pro sports. (Can anybody besides me remember sitting glued to the TV while watching the 1960 Summer Olympics broadcast from Rome?)

When it came to sports participation, however, the genders divided. The boys had more sports opportunities. Many suburban schools offered a "Gray-Y (grade school YMCA)" after-school sports program for guys. And, there were plenty of organized baseball, football, and basketball programs around.

Team sports for the girls, however, weren't quite as prevalent. There were softball and basketball after-school programs, but not nearly as frequent or as varied as today's.

Music and dance

However, Boomers of both genders and all ethic groups reported participation in – or at least awareness of – dance or music instruction in their neighborhoods.

Ballet and tap lessons were available on either an individual or group basis. And – at least for my contemporaries – 6th and 7th grade meant both genders were supposed to sign up at area dance schools for a series of "ballroom dancing" lessons. Said one guy: "I think our parents thought this might civilize us."

Music lessons for a variety of instruments were offered everywhere. The most common instrument learned was probably piano. However, in our elementary school I heard about kids taking guitar, steel guitar, organ, flute, drum, clarinet, saxophone, trumpet, French horn, tuba, and oboe instruction.

Evening plans

Boomer and his siblings – after a day of school, sports, music lessons, and so on – gather for the evening meal with Mom and Dad around 6 PM at home. Dad's working a little late today, so he doesn't get home until around 6:30. Mom's been preparing dinner about two hours. Except for canned goods and some frozen foods, she's cooked a lot of this meal from scratch.

After dinner, the family adjourns to the living room to watch their single black-and-white television. We're in the middle of the decade – let's say 1956 – so, what's on TV?

Most nights we can choose hit shows from three networks. On Sunday, nearly everybody loves the nation's top variety show "Ed Sullivan." During the rest of the week, we can select from a number of comedy/musical/variety shows, hosted by stars like Perry Como, Jack Benny, Arthur Godfrey, and Red Skelton.

There are several outstanding drama programs, like "Gunsmoke," "Alfred Hitchcock Presents" and "The Millionaire." The top-rated drama program is "General Electric Theater" hosted by future governor and President Ronald Reagan.

The year's top-rated show is one we can still see in reruns today: "I Love Lucy." *(Source for 1956–1957 movie ratings: www.fiftiesweb.com.)*

Weekends

Saturday often includes grocery or hardware store shopping for the entire family. Since this is the 1950's, there's a division of labor by gender. Mom and the daughters do household chores like cooking and cleaning, and Dad and the sons do yard work.

Shopping generally ends early, since many retailers close at 5 or 6 PM. A recent store development is "shopping centers," a group of stores connected by covered walkways, or even a mall, which includes a number of stores under one roof.

Many Jewish families go to worship on Saturday, while most Christian families go to services on Sunday. (Most stores are closed on Sunday.)

On Friday or Saturday evenings, families or teens' entertainment includes high school sporting events, roller rinks, bowling alleys, movies, and drive-ins (where recent films can be viewed from the car).

Drive-ins are sometimes called "passion pits," because they offer a place young couples can sit in cars and pretend to watch movies while they smooch.

What did we learn?

1. In Boomer days most of the nation followed the same school schedule. This made it easier to schedule summer and holiday vacations.

2. Lots of Boomers told us they spent huge amounts of time in outdoor activities. That's not the case anymore.

3. Family dining experiences have changed considerably. While most meals in Boomer days were at home, a huge number today are eaten away from the house. And, dinnertimes aren't as formal anymore.

4. Dishwashers, clothes washers, and dryers have lightened the load for both genders. And many say the microwave is one of the top three inventions of the 20th century.

5. In my personal travel region, there are still many places to buy gas...but only one full service gas station.

6. Many high schools now allow students to eat off-campus. And in many households, everybody's too busy to make sack lunches.

7. Children of Boomers still take music and dance lessons, but many are not allowed to walk or ride bicycles to and from school because of personal security issues.

8. A major positive difference in the last 50 years: Sports parity now exists for young ladies. They now have great opportunities in a variety of school and college sports.

9. Few Boomers talked much about sharing the evening meal as a family. Perhaps that's related to longer parent work schedules, more student homework, or the number of recreational opportunities that exist today.

10. The TV variety show – tremendously popular in the 1950's and 1960's – is now an infrequent television format.

11. "I Love Lucy" was – and is – one of the greatest television shows ever written.

12. Movie drive-ins are few and far between. Many say the large real estate acreage they occupied could be more profitably used for other things. That's sad.

Chapter 6
What happened in elementary school?

Thirty-plus years out of the classroom, former students still remember distinct smells, sights, and even where they sat in the auditorium. Can you do the same?

Let me confess that this "school memories" section is NOT scientific. The only people I interviewed for this were friends...some a little older, some younger. The goal is to rekindle your own memories, which are probably much the same as ours.

The early grades

My buddies claim the first thing they recall is kindergarten. Not anything specific, really...just jumbled memories of being very little in a very big room.

"I think we sat on the floor, on pillows, a lot of the time," somebody said. "And I remember rhythm band, were the teacher would play a record and we'd try to keep time to it with little triangles, wood blocks, bells, and sandpaper."

The lunchroom played a big part in a little kid's day. It divided the instructional time, and gave us our first practice at conversation.

Our lunchroom alternated between loud and deathly silent. When the kids got too loud, one of the teachers turned off the lights, which meant we had to stop talking. After a couple of minutes she'd turn them back on, and we could go back to our usual blabber.

4th, 5th, and 6th grades

My friends remember new freedom as they moved into their later elementary years. "I think we got three 'outside' breaks during the day," one friend recalls. "We had some sort of structured physical education class in the morning, an outside break right after lunch, and a 20 or 30-minute recess in the afternoon. Man, we were out playing ball all the time."

At phys ed – where guys mixed with girls – we sometimes played dodge ball. There were big circles on the pavement, and class members stood on the outside of the circle. Inside were eight kids, who dodged big volleyballs coming at them from different directions. This could be fairly dangerous.

During recess most guys played softball or kickball, and the girls – who were required to wear dresses – played jacks, raced each other, or just sat around and talked. (Those were the days of real equality...not!)

The first dances

Many classmates remember teachers instructing us in various dances, especially square dance. "I remember bowing to my partner, linking arms, and sidestepping back and forth until I was blue in the face," one guy laughs. "I never did learn to do those steps, and I never used those skills again."

But those teachers probably had another motive. They wanted to get the children used to being with members of the opposite sex, which would hopefully help them in later years.

As my class moved into 6th grade, we begin to receive formal invitations from local ballroom dancing schools. The parents encouraged this. The girls seemed to be for it. The guys weren't real sure, but we were told it would "build our character"...whatever that meant.

What did we learn?

1. Before we can learn anything, we must first create an orderly environment. That's not always easy, especially if the kid in the next desk just threw up on your shoes.

2. Age and seniority has its privileges. Any kid who doubted this found out differently if he cut in front of an older kid in lunch line.

3. It's helpful to get along with people of both sexes. If dancing class did nothing else for us, it taught us how to make small talk about things we didn't care about.

4. The school lunch line taught us to wait our turn, and to "choose responsibly" when it came to foods and beverages.

5. Athletic skills – or lack of them – became apparent to both us and our friends. Boys who displayed exceptional athletic abilities often became heroes to both male and female classmates.

CHAPTER 7
How we rated grades...
and teachers

No, no...our favorite grade is not "A-plus." I'm talking Boomers' favorite school grade. By a tiny margin, focus group members selected fourth grade.

Not surprisingly, several panelists picked the quality of the year by how much they liked the teacher. Let's listen to what they said:

"My favorite was probably 2nd grade," said A.T. "I had great playmates that I still call my friends today. I busted my lip open in class and got to go home early after bleeding on my teacher's dress.

"I was thoroughly in love with a guy, who never returned my affection...but rejection didn't mean much then. I had a bicycle and roamed free, unafraid and unmolested. My brother and sister hadn't yet decided that I was unworthy of their attention. It was a great life!"

T.C. also voted for 2nd grade. "I had the same teacher I'd had in first grade. It was finally comfortable, not new or scary."

"It was 4th grade," P.M. recalled. "I had a man teacher who was so fun, and he wanted to start an elementary school track team. He got the fourth grade girls to try out. We had a relay team with eight stations, and went to the public schools' football field and ran track meets against other elementary schools. It was the most fun time, and my first competitive sports experience."

R.R. also ranked 4th grade tops. "It was the only year in elementary school I had classes in different rooms with different teachers. I loved social studies, where we learned about different places in the world.

"My guess is that in this grade my brain was at its best for grabbing and retaining, like a sponge. So much of everything I remembered I absorbed…and more amazingly, I remember them to this day."

"My 4th grade teacher was a hottie," D.H. said. "All the other grades seemed to be mired in a kind of unpleasant lack of self-awareness. Probably fourth grade was too…but she made that year palatable."

"Fifth grade," voted D.L. "None of the worries like graduating to middle school, or the pressure to have an official girlfriend. We were at the top of the food chain. Class seemed very easy, and I had an older, experienced teacher who let us get by with way too much."

Getting older

"In 5th grade my parents took me on two education trips, the first one a historically rich tour of Boston, New York, Philadelphia, and Washington, D.C." L.H. remembered. "On the second trip I got to go to Mexico City."

"I liked 6th grade best," said D.C. "I made straight A's, played all sports, and joined Boy Scouts. I was captain of the patrol boys. And I really liked my teacher."

High school years

"My favorite was 9th grade because, at that time, it was the last grade in junior high, and I had a great time that year as a 'senior,' J.D. emphasized.

Said E.A.: "My favorite grade was sophomore year. I got freedom with a driver's license, I belonged to a school social club, I had a boyfriend, and I made good grades. I always had a great relationship with Mom and Dad, and they didn't give me a hard time because I was a good kid."

"Sophomore year – my first year in high school," agreed K.L. "I thought everything was possible and feared nothing."

"In 10th grade I could drive my Model A to school, and there was very little pressure about the future," added L.A.

"In 12th grade I had a great group of friends… two girls and five guys who hung out together daily and every weekend," remembered D.S. "We had great philosophical discussions and built lifetime friendships."

That last year of high school presented unlimited opportunity, noted M.H. "I had good classes that for once weren't too hard, a nice boyfriend with a great car, a date every weekend, and I was about to go to college."

16 things that made teachers special

What teacher do you remember best? Our panel revealed several characteristics that made their best teachers memorable:

1. "She treated the subjects of art and music as if they were just as important as all the other subjects."

2. "My journalism teacher believed in me, and made me editor of the newspaper. She was always the best sport with the students."

3. "My history teacher was the first guy I know to have said 'The reason we study history is because it repeats itself.'"

4. "My English teacher's lectures held my attention, and I respected her and her knowledge of the subject. She also taught me to write fairly well, and she stressed grammar."

5. "He made American history come alive by giving us scavenger hunt assignments to find and document various historical places right in our home town."

6. "My government and history teacher inspired me to choose a career in politics."

7. "My history teacher had a great sense of history as well as a great sense of humor."

8. "I'll always remember my 5th grade teacher, who came to see me when I represented my elementary school in the district spelling bee. He must've gotten a substitute to come in so he could be there to watch me spell. When I came in second – which meant I still advanced to the regional bee -- he gave me a great big hug."

9. "My history teacher's class on the Civil War was the most unique...it was like attending a soap opera. You left each day wanting to come back soon for the next installment."

10. "My French teacher thought I was wonderful, and would have named me best French student except some BOY had a fraction of a higher grade in French than I did."

11. "My history teacher was smart as a whip, challenging, and a real smart aleck. I even visited her in later years after she moved to another city."

12. "My drama teacher inspired me to my career path."

13. "In high school I loved my sewing teacher. I took the course for three years and got to be a model at a teachers' association style show. I went to college wanting to be just like that teacher."

14. "My 6th grade teacher was the best overall. Somehow he was able to make each and every one of us believe we were his favorite."

15. "My first grade teacher was the sweetest woman who seemed to genuinely love the children she taught. When I was a child I was painfully shy, but this dear teacher was the one who brought me out, showed me there was no reason to be afraid, and helped me enjoy school."

16. "My English teacher not only taught the subject, but gave us great advice about getting along in the world. Examples: 'Get it in writing' and 'Always listen to the other side of the story so you'll know what you're talking about in an argument, and who the enemy is.'"

What did we learn?

1. Our panel felt that – during childhood – it's darn near divine to be nine and in fourth grade.

2. Elementary school years were a highlight for many Boomers. They formed lifelong friendships, and experienced the freedom of almost unrestricted bicycle travel within the immediate neighborhood.

3. In elementary years, some reported their ability to absorb and retain great amounts of information.

4. During middle school, two said that travel opportunities broadened their thinking, and made them historically aware.

5. High school and drivers' licenses gave Boomers a sense of upcoming adulthood. College offered several the feeling of great opportunity.

6. Our favorite elementary school teachers genuinely cared about us, helped us overcome shyness, took special interest in our activities, and convinced us that we were among their favorite students.

7. Our favorite English teachers stressed the importance of grammar, and taught us the value of writing and communicating well.

8. Our favorite history teachers reminded us that we could find important historical sites near our homes, that history often repeats itself, that this subject could be presented dramatically and relevantly, and that it could inspire us to careers in public service.

9. Our favorite language, drama, art, music, homemaking, business, and journalism teachers reminded us that great satisfaction can come from learning special skills.

CHAPTER 8
Favorite games and toys for girls and boys

My wife and I come home each evening to a house fully-plugged into the 21st century. We sit at computers and play online games, turn on the TV to compete in interactive virtual sports, or slip in a DVD to watch the latest movie.

Our daughter, a recent college grad, keeps us up-to-date on emerging technology. And we've got lots of young relatives who provide us instant answers to our middle-aged questions.

That's a far cry from our games of the mid-20th century. But many of them are still around, a tribute to the forward thinking of those creative inventors.

It's "flashback" time now. We asked our focus group members what they did with their free time, and here's what they told us.

What guys said (games/sports listed alphabetically)

Baseball – Popular as a sandlot game, as a parent-supported organized activity, and as a television sport. A few vividly recalled the Saturday "Game of the Week" with Dizzy Dean and Pee Wee Reese. Two recalled a favorite baseball glove.

Baseball cards – Many Boomer boys remember collecting these cards – with the player's face on one side and the prior years' statistics on the other – for several years. Opening a package of baseball cards to find a superstar player inside was the pre-teen equivalent to winning the lottery.

Basketball

Bicycle – Probably the most frequently-named possession. Some specifically mentioned owning a Schwinn bicycle. One Boomer talked about the bicycle motocross popularity of the 1970's. (Boomers' purchases of multi-speed bicycles from the late 1960's through the 1970's triggered a worldwide "bike boom.")

Cap pistols – Great for chasing friends or firing at make-believe bandits. "I had Roy Rogers pearl-handled cap pistols," one Boomer proudly told us.

Climbing trees – Is this a sport, a game, or what? Whatever, it's stored forever in Boomer's memories. One person mentioned a "neighborhood tree," where each child occupied a specific limb or branch.

Clue – The classic board game.

Davy Crockett/Daniel Boone – Many products like raccoon skin caps, toy hunting rifles, and fringed shirts and pants were purchased by fans who wanted to be like these pioneer heroes.

Dodge ball – There are several variations of this game. In one, several stand in a large circle. Some participants stand inside the circle, while those on the outside attempt to hit them with a large ball. If someone on the outside of the circle hits someone on the inside, the thrower gets to go inside the circle, and the one who was hit goes to the outside.

There's another version where teams compete, and the last person left unhit by the ball wins for his/her team.

Drop the Handkerchief – Here's the exact quote from the "Pioneer Children" web site: "Players join hands and form a circle while 'it' holds a handkerchief and runs around the circle. 'It' drops the handkerchief behind one of the players and keeps running. The player then picks up the handkerchief and runs around the circle in the opposite direction. They race to see who reaches the empty spot first. The loser becomes the next 'it.'"

Football – One of Boomer boys' favorite games, as were its equipment like helmets and pads. Several recalled informal pass-and-catch games, or two vs. two games.

Glider, balsa wood – These ultra-light planes were available in several sizes.

Jigsaw puzzles

Machine gun, plastic – Specifically mentioned: a World War II style Thompson submachine gun.

Monopoly – The board game named most often as the favorite in our survey.

Plastic soldiers – A huge favorite among Boomers. They could be purchased in toy or five-and-dime stores. Most were about 2"-3" long, in a variety of action poses.

Softball

Teddy bear

Train set, electric – "I still have my Lionel set," one Boomer told us.

What girls said

Barbie – One of the most popular dolls – and toys – of all time. "I was a pretty typical little girl," A.T. reported. "I loved Barbie and had tons of her pink paraphernalia, like the Barbie Dream House and her three-wheel ATV, not to mention all the clothes and accessories. Whenever I'd lose one of Barbie's little high heel shoes, my poor Dad always found it in the shag carpeting when it imbedded itself in his heel."

Chemistry set – "My cousin had one," J.D. remembered, "which we successfully blew up."

Dolls – In addition to Barbie, there are too many names and types to list. But if you were a Boomer, you probably know them. "Saucy Walker, Besty Wetsy, Madame Alexander, Tiny Tears, Ginny…those were my dolls," one Boomer reported.

Fall – "This was a hairpiece that I tucked under my short, fine fringe of hair," said E.F. "Never before or since have I been able to toss my hair and wear headbands. I have lots of pictures with that hairpiece I thought looked so good."

Four Square – Four players stand in four separate interconnecting squares, and score points by how they bounce a ball in their opponents' square.

Hopscotch – Several schools had permanent hopscotch squares pained on their asphalted or cemented areas.

Horseback riding – Even in large urban areas, one could often find stables where customers could "rent" a gentle riding horse for an hour or two.

Hula Hoops – These incredible large hoops are a perennial favorite with both genders.

Jacks – A favorite game of elementary and middle school girls. It generally required at least six jacks and either a golf ball or small rubber ball. "Now about the jacks," explained J.H. "You were a true 'L7' (that would be a square) if you played with six jacks. The term would be 'dork' today. Ten jacks was a minimum! At the end of the first round – onsies, twosies etc.– we would take turns calling out the next game…double bouncies, pigs in the barn, around the world and so on."

Jump rope, Double Dutch – This quote comes directly from Wikipedia: "Double Dutch is a sport in which one person jumps rope with two ropes, and one or more people jumping simultaneously. Playing Double Dutch involves at least three people total: one or more jumping and two turning the ropes. A person jumping usually does tricks that may involve gymnastics or breakdancing; it can also have fancy foot movements incorporated. Young people, including many boys, do this for fitness, and it is competed at world level. Competitions in double-dutch were often seen at block parties."

Kick the Can – This is a little bit like hide-and-seek.

Nancy Drew books – This book series was – and remains – popular among young ladies. "I established my own Nancy Drew Detective Agency when I was in third grade," one lady told us.

Record player – Those of us over 40 often find it hard to describe either large stereo systems or portable record players to our children. Even harder to describe are the different turntable cycles required to play 33-1/3, 45, and 78 rpm records.

Red Rover – This game requires two teams. Each team holds hands. The first team chooses an opposing team's player to attempt to break through their line by saying "Red Rover, Red Rover, let (person's name) come over." If that person breaks through the line, he then becomes part of that team. The other team then picks a player. (I'm not sure how this game ends.)

Roller skating – A few talked about large birthday parties at area roller rinks. There were also sidewalk skates.

Steal the Bacon – In this game there are two teams and an umpire. Each team member is assigned a number. An object ("the bacon") is placed in between them. The umpire calls out a number, and team members with that number attempt to be the first to grab the bacon and return it to their side without being touched (tagged) by a member of the other team.

Swimming – Most kids loved summers spent either paddling about in the water, or playing various swimming pool games.

Track – "When I got to fourth grade," recalled P.M., "the only man teacher in the school started a track team. Girls and boys ran relay races against other schools, and it was the best time."

Twister – Many of us loved this game played on a large plastic floor covering which displayed various colored circles. Each player received instructions from a spinner on where to place each of his/her feet and hands.

Wahoo – Again, this direct quote comes from Wikipedia: "Wahoo, a game similar to HYPERLINK "http://en.wikipedia.org/wiki/Parchisi" \o "Parchisi" Parchisi, is a board game that involves moving a set number of marbles around the board, trying to get them into the safety zone. Most boards are four to six players. Wahoo has been a popular game for decades."

What did we learn?

1. Several participants expressed regret that citizens don't spend leisure hours outside any more. One speculated that this insular lifestyle has contributed to neighborhood decline.

2. Many Boomer games required several participants and constant interaction and mediation, a skill much needed today.

3. Disturbing news reports make today's responsible parents wary of outside dangers, and inhibit the free lifestyle most of us reportedly experienced.

4. Many boys' toys were weapons: toy cowboys, soldiers, guns, and knives. Some attribute this to the number of western and war series telecast in the 1950's and 1960's.

5. A number of television programs dramatized alternately the American frontier and the American cowboy, or futuristic space age themes. Were we seeking to move forward too fast, and simultaneously attributing more value to the past?

CHAPTER 9
How to get by in junior high

Somewhere between the ages of 12 and 15 we Boomers survived another crisis: junior high school. Remember that?

Some of us grew tall. Some didn't grow at all. Some grew beards, including some of the guys. And for at least six months – and for a few of us three years – we drifted thorough that awkward period when we tripped, stumbled, or misspoke over and over.

Kids still experience the same trauma, but today there's much better medication. Even unexpected pimple break-outs can be treated quickly.

But what experiences during those middle years shaped us? By gossiping with old friends, I've uncovered several:

1. Gender awakening – Perhaps for the first time we began to pay attention to the opposite sex. Girls – who matured earlier – seemed ahead of the guys. The boys who spent all their free time talking sports now began to consider other pastimes.
2. Skill development – We began to see that some classmates were much better than others at specific tasks. In fact, some classmates were truly gifted.

"I remember competing in baseball with one phenomenal player," a Boomer said. "This dude didn't play the same game the rest of us did. For one thing, he was bigger, with powerful arms and wrists.

"The most unusual thing about him was his eyes. Most of us just watched the pitcher throw the ball, then took a swing. This dude could follow it all the way to the plate, and could smack it into any field." What happened to him?

"Major leagues," the Texas Boomer said. "Then coaching. His substantial abilities helped define his future."

Other students began to catch teachers' attention in math, science, and writing. Their natural gifts set them apart. Only time would tell if they developed them fully.

3. Social networking – Somebody once said that "junior high school is the place where social networks are born." During this three-year journey we learned that (a) the friends we chose defined us, (b) the clothes styles we selected – or neglected – created prejudices among peers, and (c) the causes we embraced isolated us from certain segments of our class.

4. Values – This is the place where we began defining ours. (a) Financially, we began to see where our family's income fell in relation to our peers. (b) Educationally, we noticed that some classmates had instructional advantages that others did not. For example, a math professor's children might have been learning math concepts from an early

age, allowing them to stand out in class. (c) Physically, we began to perceive that good looks or body build were simply luck in the genetic draw. But we also noticed that these attributes gave certain individuals advantages over others.

Chapter 10
Did you have these thoughts in high school?

How did you feel the first day of your freshman year? Some people say this is the most confusing day of their lives. Among thoughts that run through their heads as they walk through the halls:

1. Confusion and despair as they try to navigate a strange new building.
2. Fear of upperclassmen, teachers, coaches, administration.
3. Anxiety – Will they succeed in this larger, institutional, and sometimes threatening environment?
4. Anticipation of new activities including sports, music, art, and social clubs.
5. Separation from parents and family as they enter their first semi-adult environment.

No doubt about it. High school is significant. And, somebody famous once said, "It's the one uniquely American rite of passage nearly all of us share."

Today, three-plus decades after graduation, most Boomers remember it as "a time of confusion. I didn't know who I was, "one guy moaned, "and I considered my problems to be totally unique, so I didn't share them with anyone. If I had, I would have discovered nearly all of us were feeling the same way."

You and I had different high school experiences. Most of us belonged to some sort of social group – either school-sponsored or informal – during those years. Did you participate in any of the following?

1. Football/basketball/baseball – These major sports were predominantly male during our years. Today, of course, basketball and softball are also major girls' sports.
2. Tennis/volleyball/track – While these sports didn't draw as many spectators, they attracted a number of good athletes of both genders.
3. Band/orchestra/chorus – Those of us with musical talents may have participated here.
4. ROTC – Some have told me their high school experience helped them in college ROTC, and later in the military.
5. Newspaper/yearbook – For many students this was a prestigious group. They could write about their friends, and gather great school gossip.
6. Art – A few people told me their participation in art and design forged a future career path.
7. Distributive education – If you participated here, you likely went to school for one-half day and worked the other half. Many used these classes to obtain state certification as hairstylists, barbers, mechanics, draftsmen, and several other specialties.
8. Future Homemakers, Future Business Leaders, etc. – These clubs attracted students who wanted to learn more about specific careers.

Often, professionals in that career field would visit the students to tell them more about their professions.

9. Social clubs – These were often sort of pre-college fraternities or sororities. Many were not sanctioned by schools. Many were not allowed to meet on campus. They were, however, powerful social mechanisms.

Mary, a mid-50's Boomer, says she also recalls that the women of this age group were "caught between two societies. The women of our parents' generation mostly believed that ladies stayed at home, cared for their children, and put the priorities of the husband first.

"However, the age group 10 to 15 years ahead of us was redefining females. They wanted traditionally male careers to be available to them. They wanted equal pay for equal work. They wanted to decide if they wanted children or not.

"What were we – the Baby Boom generation – to do? As it turned out, some of us took both paths. It's really different for our daughters. They live in a much more accepting society."

What did we learn?

1. Most of us felt out of place and lonely in high school. Later, we found out that just about everybody else did, too.

2. Our friends and extracurricular events helped define us on the ever-changing high school popularity scale.

3. Some said high school was the most difficult and painful period of their lives.

4. It's virtually impossible to keep up with friends after high school. Many do not reconnect until the 20th year class reunion!

5. Women of the Boomer generation are probably the first to be offered a wide choice of career opportunities.

Chapter 11
Rags, wheels, and other teen trends

In the beginning – at least in OUR beginnings – there was a dress code. Elders wore work and dress clothes prescribed by society. A medical professional wore a certain apparel…a businessman wore another.

This continued throughout most of the 1950's. Then something happened, actually even before the oldest Baby Boomers came of age. Teen guys began to grow their hair a little longer, and mix tee-shirts with blue jeans and leather jackets to create a "rebellious look."

Some claim Elvis or James Dean or Marlon Brando started the look. Others blamed everything on that new music, rock-and-roll.

But by the time the first Boomers landed on high school soil, teens had adopted a specific look, jargon-laden language, and unique preferences for everything from cars to cafés.

Cool clothes/girls

"What I remember are hot pants and hot polyester," J.H. laughs.

"I remember those mid-60's oxford cloth button-down collar shirts," said one Boomer. "Also, there was a lot of madras, and – for shoes – loafers."

"Bleeding madras shirts," echos R.R. "Even madras swim trunks, which were outlawed because they bled in the swimming pools. Paisley prints were also popular."

"Now, we've seen a resurgence of paisley and bleeding madras plaid...probably people our age in the clothing industry recycling things we liked when we were kids."

"Madras, madras, madras," said G.M. "I also succumbed to frosting my hair in college, like all my sorority sisters."

"There was lots of big hair on girls," laughed K.L., referring to sprayed-and-teased hairstyles. "Also, there were mini-skirts in the 1960's, and clothing looks copied from teens who appeared on American Bandstand."

"In high school," P.M. recalled, "girls still had to wear dresses or skirts to class. We wore socks and penny loafer shoes with them. Every girl wanted loafers.

"In college, times began to change to a 'flower child' era, and those clothes were wild, with bright colors and great color combinations.

"The skirts just got shorter and shorter, and the pants became hip-huggers with bell-bottom cuffs."

"I remember mini-skirts, and all the psychedelic colors and clothes. What a fun time to go to school," J.D. said.

"Other girls' styles?" asked D.S. "I also remember bell bottom jeans, halter tops, baby doll blouses, and pierced ears."

"Clothing changed drastically in the late 1960's from very conservative to 'flower child,'" said J.J.

The 'preppy' look

"There was one movement that flourished when I was 14 or 15 that I utterly detested, and still do," said one younger Boomer. "I had friends who lived or died by 'The Preppy Handbook,' including a friend since kindergarten who embraced the style so wholeheartedly that I still refer to her as 'lotta plaid Suzie.'

"Loafer shoes, khakis, madras shorts and skirts, polo shirts, and the eponymous navy blazer. One dear friend had a much-envied pair of moccasin-style shoes in pink and lime green that won her the title of 'Preppiest Girl on Campus' our freshman year.

"My answer to this? Shopping for camouflage pants at a nearby surplus store."

"Anything preppy," said T.C., another younger Boomer. "I also remember fashions from the movie 'Flashdance' when we were in college."

Cool clothes/guys

Oxford cloth, button-down collar shirts, madras shirts, walking shorts, and windbreakers, and penny loafers were named as the informal school "uniform" of the early and mid-1960's. "There was clothing sameness among our peers," said D.J.

"I remember wearing washed-out Levi's, white athletic socks with black loafers – which never had taps – and going to either a drive-in hamburger place or drive-in movie looking cool," said A.L.

"I never cared much for fads," added L.H., "but I did enjoy wearing the Navy pea jacket I bought at the Army surplus store."

"Guy clothes changed big-time in the late 1960's and early 1970's," noted another older Boomer. "We wore older jeans, more tee-shirts, more wild prints and wide, open-collared shirts," W.R. said. "We wore more boots and moccasins, or loafers without socks. We went for more of a 'grubby but cool' appearance."

"Three movies influenced clothing in my teen years," said D.L., a younger Boomer. The first was John Travolta in 'Saturday Night Fever' when I was in middle school. Then the big one, John Travolta in 'Urban Cowboy' in 1981.

"Then, in college, we revisited the 1978 classic movie 'Animal House' with John Belushi when I joined a fraternity in 1984."

Other nifty stuff

"I loved my 1967 Camaro 327," remembered E.A. "Those cars were all the rage, and I kept it until I got a 1973 Mercury Capri. It's interesting that I keep cars longer now than I did back in my early single working days."

"Remarkably, one of my favorite fads is still around," added F.K. "It's stereo – not monaural – music."

"Did anybody mention the Hula Hoop, dancing the Twist, and Mod clothing?" asked R.H. "Those were major fads." Mod clothing, you may remember, was inspired by popular British music groups who dominated American music in the mid-1960's.

"Long hair was a major item for both girls and boys," said D.C. "Also – for a short time in the 1970's – streaking (running naked) was big."

"It would be hard to overestimate the influence of rock 'n roll," added another older Boomer. "There was also a big transition in dancing for us, from ballroom dance classes to the Twist."

"Did anybody mention hair bleaching?" asked A.V. "That was big for both girls and boys. "I got my hair bleached the day before my grandfather's funeral. Sorry, Mom."

"Don't forget ping pong and table shuffleboard," concluded D.J.

What did we learn?

1. Boomers first expressed our differences with previous generations by completely changing clothing styles and rules of conformity.

2. Longer hair – perhaps copied from the style of 1950's rock-and-rollers or from popular British rock groups – became a generational standard and a protest against early 1960's conformity.

3. Car styles changed drastically from year to year, and were wisely marketed to this country's largest generation. During those decades, most teens and young adults chose American cars.

4. In the midst of the "hippie" decade there was a return to the "preppie" look, which utilized many styles of the 1950's and early 1960's. From that time forward, clothing choices became more individually taste-regulated then prescribed by society.

5. Many Boomers who expressed the most visible and liberal lifestyle changes in early adulthood have become the most conservative in raising their own children.

Chapter 12
Boomers talk about their best friends

Best friends are priceless. They listen to your problems, they offer solutions, you listen to their problems, you offer solutions. You learn and grow together.

That's why we asked our focus group what they most admired about their best friends. Here's what they told us:

Sense of humor – "My elementary friend was a sweetheart with a great sense of humor. In high school, my best friend was shy, smart, and tall. Although she was shy, she had a super-silly sense of humor and was totally boy-crazy – just like me."

Cut-up – "In elementary, my friend and I were all about fun, laughter, and cutting up. In high school, my best friend and I were all about belonging to something, and not getting beat up. He was also a help with girls."

Loves to laugh – "In elementary, my friend lived a couple of blocks away from my house, and was a tomboy like me. In high school, it was a cheerleader who had perfect silky straight hair, perfect complexion, and a straight-A student with a red convertible Volkswagen who rode horses on weekends and loved to laugh."

Cub Scouts buddies – "My Cub Scout group was my pack of good friends. We attended the same school, and have stayed in touch all these years."

Camp Fire friends – "In elementary, I had lots of friends and maybe not really a best friend. I loved my Bluebird and Camp Fire Girl group, and we all did so much together. In high school my very best friend had to get married and drop out of school. It broke my heart, and we tried to keep our friendship together, but we no longer had very much in common."

Loyal – "In elementary school she was outgoing, popular, fun-loving, and smart. My high school friend was smart, pretty, loyal, but lacked self-confidence."

Sports participants – "In elementary school we had a group that played sports together all the time, which I would describe as being like the Little Rascals on television. In high school they were in a band with me."

Shared blame – "My best friend in elementary was the one I could always blame for getting me in trouble. By the time I reached high school I ran out of friends on whom to lay the blame."

Popular – "In elementary we kind of traded off being friends with different groups. In high school she was popular, and I vicariously enjoyed her popularity. She was fun to hang out with, and her parents accepted me like a second daughter as I spent lots of time at their house. She was kind and smart and funny. I have great memories of times spent with her spending the night, playing the player piano and singing, or riding around in one of our cars."

Had a car – "He was the same best friend in elementary and high school. He was the first one to have a car – two years before I did – so it was good to get around in."

Shared activities – "In elementary, she was very shy, and I had to learn how not to hurt her feelings. In high school, I didn't have just one best friend…I had a great friend in each area – church, art class, high school clubs – that interested me."

Integrity – "My best friend in elementary and high school was the same guy. He was quiet, thoughtful, and of high integrity."

Imagination – "My elementary best friend was tiny and dark-haired with a little freckled snub nose. She was full of imagination, and had a home and yard that encouraged our creative games. She also had a much higher threshold for scary movies and stories than I did. I frequently was frightened out of my mind by her and her brother, who liked to jump out of dark corners at me.

"In high school, my best friend and I were on the swim team together, and would 'carbo-load' on chili burgers and fries before a meet. Her folks gave her a Camaro for her 16th birthday, and she was the envy of all."

Opposites – "In elementary, my best friend looked the opposite in just about every way. She had translucent white skin, blonde hair and big blue eyes, dressed beautifully, and had delicate hands with long fingernails. I had deeply sun-kissed skin, dark brown hair and eyes, and badly bitten fingernails. I guess it was just a case of 'opposites attract.'

"In middle and high school I had the same best buddy. We spent every day after school at her house studying and listening to her older sister's Johnny Mathis records. We had a little group of gals who ran around together, sat at the same lunch table, and liked boys. It never caused any trouble among us, though. I wish I kept in touch with her after graduation, but as things go, everyone got busy with living their lives."

What did we learn?

1. Most people told us their best friends made them feel good about themselves, or helped them laugh.

2. Some elementary school buddies became lifelong friends. In other cases, friends changed as individuals moved into high school and developed different interests.

3. Loyalty and integrity among friends is critical.

4. Sharing blame with a friend often built loyalty.

5. Interest in the same activities in both elementary and high school often built friendships.

6. Car acquisition was a major deal. It marked the beginning of adulthood freedom. If we didn't have a car, we wanted access to friends who did.

7. Vivid imaginations led to exciting after-school adventures and dreams.

8. The belief that a friend is more popular than we are may attract us to them.

9. Opposites often attract, in friendships as well as marriage.

10. It's extremely difficult to maintain school friendships once we leave that environment.

Chapter 13
Our favorite books:
leafing through literature

We Boomers are a literary bunch. We learned to read early. And after we got older, lots of us read and watched television at the same time.

Since 50 Boomers were invited to join our focus group, we received lots of book recommendations. Here are a few books our group read and enjoyed, listed alphabetically:

A Christmas Carol by Charles Dickens
A Connecticut Yankee in King Arthur's Court by Mark Twain
Adventures of Mabel by Harry Thurston Peck
A Farewell to Arms by Ernest Hemmingway
A Fairly Honorable Defeat by Iris Murdoch
All the King's Men by Robert Penn Warren
Amuse Ourselves to Death by Neil Postman
Animal Farm by George Orwell
Anne of Green Gables by Lucy Maud Montgomery
Are You There, God? It's Me, Margaret by Judy Bloom
Atlas Shrugged by Ayn Rand
Ben-Hur by Lew Wallace
Black Beauty by Anna Sewell
Black Stallion book series by Walter Farley
Bridge at Andau by James Michener

Call of the Wild by Jack London

Catcher in the Rye by J.D. Salinger

Charlotte's Web by E.B. White

Chip Hilton (sports book series) by Clair Bee

Death Be Not Proud by John Gunther

Fail Safe by Eugene Burdick and Harvey Wheeler

Gone with the Wind by Margaret Mitchell

Hardy Boys mysteries by Franklin W. Dixon

Helen Keller – "Anything about her. I thought she was amazing," one Boomer wrote.

Huckleberry Finn by Mark Twain

Jane Eyre by Charlotte Bronte'

Little House on the Prairie by Laura Ingalls Wilder

Little Men by Louisa May Alcott

Little Women by Louisa May Alcott

Macbeth by William Shakespeare

Michael Strogoff: The Courier of the Czar by Jules Verne

Nancy Drew series by Carolyn Keene

Of Mice and Men by John Steinbeck

Old Man and the Sea by Ernest Hemingway

Once and Future King by T.H. White

Peter Rabbit by Beatrix Potter

Portnoy's Complaint by Philip Roth

Portrait of the Artist as a Young Man by James Joyce

Prince and the Pauper by Mark Twain

Rebecca and the King's General by Dame Daphne DuMaurier

Secret of the Old Clock – A Nancy Drew mystery.

Scarlet Letter by Nathaniel Hawthorne
Shepherd of the Hills by Harold Bell Wright
Stuart Little, which was reportedly E.B. White's first children's story.
Sue Barton (nurse series) by Helen Dore Boylston
Tale of Two Cities by Charles Dickens
This Side of Paradise by F. Scott Fitzgerald
Time Machine by H.G. Wells
Tom Sawyer by Mark Twain

What did we learn?

1. Many of us loved to read books about animals who displayed noble or human characteristics like Animal Farm, Charlotte's Web, Peter Rabbit, Stuart Little, Black Beauty, and the Black Stallion.

2. We apparently enjoyed books in either a series or serial form. Boys enjoyed the Chip Hilton sports series or Hardy Boys mysteries. Girls enjoyed Little Men, Little Women, Little House on the Prairie, the Nancy Drew detective books, and the Sue Barton series about nurses.

3. Many Boomers were drawn to action or mystery books.

4. Several enjoyed "coming of age" or "growing up" books like Portrait of the Artist as a Young Man, Are You There, God? It's Me, Margaret and – a huge favorite among teens – Catcher in the Rye.

5. One mild surprise: Although we grew up in an era of space emphasis and exploration, the only "futuristic" novel chosen by a panel member was The Time Machine.

CHAPTER 14
Why Boomers squeeze time: the compression factor

OK, Boomers, here's a sad admission from one of your own: I try to constrict two minutes' worth of activity into every minute of each waking hour. I admit this freely because (a) I want to do a lot of things before my heart stops, and (b) a bunch of you have told me the same thing.

Why are we like this? Maybe it's because we were raised during a time when adults who grew up during the Depression sought to improve their lives in the 1950's and 1960's.

In large numbers, they subscribed to more magazines, and joined book and record clubs in an effort to continue their educations, and pursue new interests.

"I had loads of stuff to read," recalled W.R. "My parents, aunts and uncles, and grandparents subscribed to lots of magazines, and my grandmother received periodic condensed books of best-sellers. What a concept! One could sit down and – in only a few hours – be up-to-date on the modern classics."

Even young readers could understand great novels, the latest detective thriller, or serious history if stories were delivered to them in short, digestible packages.

Early reading habits

A few said their voracious reading activities were initially nurtured in first grade. Reading began – for many of us – with the word list.

We memorized a bunch of words printed on a large chart, or on the blackboard. Then, the teacher could stack these now-recognizable letter combinations into simple sentences and – suddenly – we could READ!

Next, these simple words were grouped with pictures of complex items like a BIRDBATH or AIRPLANE or BULLDOZER. We had books combining letters and pictures together, which simultaneously built our vocabulary while telling a simple story. What a genius idea!

Then, we got exposed to another narrative format few of us could resist. What was it?

The comic book!

"There were five kids in my family," J.A. remembered. "Every summer we spent several weeks visiting our grandparents. My grandmother bought loads of comic books for us.

"Those books got handled so much, she began to stitch the spines with thread so we could continue reading them. Wow, we had hundred of those books! The stories were exciting, simple, and vividly illustrated.

"At a family reunion recently, we began to talk about those great stories. Nobody remembers what happened to them…but I sure wish we had them back."

What did we learn?

1. "Compression" thinking – In this busy age, we should try to limit our e-mails and other correspondence to a single page.

2. Reinforce one theme – Simple, basic ideas can be communicated easily. Everything else in e-mails, memos or letters – including the P.S. – should reinforce a single idea. (Remember the first stories we read?)

3. Instant knowledge – When we Boomers want to communicate, we need to present the information succinctly. Consider short words, sentences, and paragraphs.

4. "How to" books became quite popular for our parents' generation, and continue to be popular reference volumes for Boomers, too. We welcome ways to improve our mental and professional skills.

5. Many of us – former comic book readers – sometimes like to receive verbal information coupled with graphics.

6. Shorter is often better – Think about Abe Lincoln. His Gettysburg Address, lasting only a couple minutes, contained only 286 words.

Chapter 15
Movie favorites: just pop culture, or our generation's true beliefs?

The movies our panel picked covered multiple themes. For us to come up with a single favorite from these would be impossible.

We took the easy way out. We asked our focus group what movies they liked best, and why. Then we listed them in alphabetical order, and added comments the panelists made about them.

A Summer Place – "It's my favorite movie of my entire life. I have never wavered from that. I loved the innocent romance (sort of) and the true love they found. It's corny, but I loved it and still do."

All That Jazz

Auntie Mame – (This Boomer also nominated "Gigi" and "My Fair Lady" for the same reasons.) – "These movies were great entertainment. I've seen them all multiple times. I loved the costumes, the sets, and the elegance of all three movies."

Ben-Hur – "It is the story of how Christ crossed one man's path several times during his lifetime. It is a story of survival and endurance, of circumstance, and providence." Another comment: "The chariot race is still one of the top ten action clips ever filmed." A third Boomer's quote: "I saw it because I had read the book."

Big Chill – A college favorite. "I recall having a very visceral reaction to the idea of my husband sharing DNA with my best friend. I thought, 'No way, no how.' Now I think I better understand both women's impulse – first to ask and second to agree."

Cinderella – "First Disney movie I saw was with my mother...my first time to see real COLOR! Wow!"

Butch Cassidy and the Sundance Kid

Cleopatra – "It had Elizabeth Taylor, Richard Burton, and unbelievably spectacular sets."

Cool Hand Luke

Dr. Zhivago – "What impressed me was Julie Christie." Another comment: "It was a love story, but it also had a great history lesson in it, and I loved history."

Easy Rider – "It introduced me to the counter-culture."

Flight of the Phoenix – "I like the original, with Jimmy Stewart. It tweaked my interest in aviation and international travel, and I'm still tweaked!"

Footloose – "The theme of breaking the rules when they need to be broken has been a life theme of mine."

Francis the Talking Mule

From Russia with Love – "The fight scene on the train was the first realistic fight scene I'd seen."

Giant

Gigi

Godfather

Gone with the Wind – "Nothing like it ever since, and probably never will be."

Grease – "I saw it probably 100 times the summer it came out. (It helped that I worked in a movie theater.)

I'd slip from behind the concession stand and go stand in the door of the theater. I learned all the words to all the songs; in fact, I probably still know them all." Another Boomer's comment: "Oh, to be cool and in high school!"

Goldfinger – "Of all the James Bond films, this is my pick. This suave secret agent man gets the bad guys AND the girls."

How to Marry a Millionaire – "Virna Lisi."

Invaders from Mars

Invasion of the Body Snatchers – This is my personal favorite. It's about pods from outer space who can inhabit human bodies. A small town doctor (Kevin McCarthy) discovers his friends and patients are being replaced by these other-worldly creatures. For the first time, it made me realize that things are not always what they seem…and that it is good to be skeptical.

Irma La Douce

Magnificent Seven

Manchurian Candidate – "It starred Frank Sinatra. Great filmmaking, great story."

My Fair Lady

North by Northwest – "Directed by Alfred Hitchcock, it has Eva Marie Saint, James Mason, and Cary Grant. Enough said."

Parent Trap – "The original had Hayley Mills, Brian Keith, and Maureen O'Hara. I wanted to live on a ranch with Brian Keith and swim in his pool every day. I wanted to marry him."

Pink Panther – "Really funny."

Pollyana

Red River – "It depicts a cattle drive as it most likely really was."

Rocky Horror Picture Show – "I loved an excuse to be out really late, and it was so bizarre!"

Shot in the Dark – "Superb acting."

Sound of Music – "It was special because it showed how a man without a wife and so many kids found his true love instead of the love he was originally going to marry. All of us girls wanted to be Maria and have that wedding." Another Boomer's comment: "It had great songs, a very happy ending, cute kids, romance…it kind of had it all."

Spartacus

Star Wars – "I saw it on vacation. The special effects had us all shooting lasers at imaginary space ships as we drove by familiar sights on the way home."

Tarantula

Ten Commandments – "It is a Bible story in spectacular form."

The Graduate – "It seemed to capture our generation's reaction to our parents' generation."

Them – "It was about giant ants – mutated by the nuclear tests in New Mexico – that take over the world. I was pretty young when I saw it, and it made me never trust any side effects of technology."

Thirteen Ghosts – "Excellent combination horror/science fiction/3-D movie."

To Kill A Mockingbird – "Another loss of innocence, this time regarding race. How did I go through my entire childhood without being aware of racial prejudice?"

Trapeze – "My Dad has been a Shriner. Each year the Shrine Circus would come to town, and we loved going. Dad took us to the movie theater to see 'Trapeze,' and I would have joined the circus if I could have been the star on a trapeze."

Twenty Thousand Leagues Under the Sea – "I saw it in elementary school, and thought it was really cool."

2001: A Space Odyssey – "I stopped and watched on a TV in a downtown department store when Neil Armstrong set foot on the moon. The movie had been released the year before that. I thought we were going to really do it…and would be living in space and mining asteroids by now." Another comment: "It was the ultimate science fiction movie."

Wizard of Oz – "It delivered a life lesson, 'There's no place like home,' in a brilliantly colored and brightly wrapped package." Another Boomer commented: "First it was black-and-white, then color. It had flying monkeys. Bert Lahr was fantastic. I remember the line 'Don't pay any attention to the man behind the curtain.'"

What did we learn?

1. Boomers apparently preferred dramas over comedy. Our panel picked ten drama favorites, and four in the comedy category. Even as youngsters, we may have been a serous bunch.

2. Three westerns were chosen for our list. And, a couple of Boomers commented that they loved any movie that starred John Wayne, many of which were

westerns. We may also favor westerns because so many fine ones appeared on TV in the 1950's and 1960's.

3. We classified nine movies as epics -- heroic tales of great deeds. Those included Ben-Hur, Cleopatra, Dr. Zhivago, Giant, Gone with the Wind, Spartacus, Star Wars, Ten Commandments, and Wizard of Oz.

4. Seven musicals ranked high with us, maybe because our generation's had the opportunity to hear all categories of tunes from movies, TV, and radio.

5. I classified five shows as "generational" films. In the 1950's, that meant shows like A Summer Place. In the 1960's, movies like The Graduate and Easy Rider drew distinctive differences between us and our elders. The Big Chill, made in 1983, presented early Boomers returning to their hometown to attend a friend's funeral.

Younger Boomers also experienced defining films, like Footloose and St. Elmo's Fire.

6. Several great movies – including some perennial action and animated classics – were once considered children's films. But their messages are relevant for Boomer adults, too.

7. My favorite category is horror/science fiction, a staple of our collective childhoods. Invasion of the Body Snatchers, Them, 2001: A Space Odyssey, Invaders from Mars, and Thirteen Ghosts made us fear that there are (a) terrors we cannot see, (b) life on other planets, and (c) aliens from other galaxies who may be planning a trip here.

CHAPTER 16
Best years of TV for you and me

Try to remember those olden days, Boomers. Remember when television in most cities had just three or four channels? Remember when families asked a family member – or hired a guy – to climb onto the roof to position the antenna?

Remember when TV didn't broadcast 24 hours a day? Remember what a "test pattern" looked like? Remember when you could adjust seven or eight knobs on the front of a black-and-white television (brightness, contrast, vertical and horizontal hold, etc.)?

We asked our contemporaries to tell us about shows they loved most. Here's a sampling of what they said.

Westerns and animals

Several told us they watched westerns avidly. "Sky King, Roy and Dale...too many favorites," M.F. remembered. "I used to draw down on Matt Dillon every week at the beginning of Gunsmoke. I also enjoyed Rawhide, Have Gun Will Travel, Maverick, and Wild, Wild West. The old-time cowboys bordered on the mythological, and the later ones – like Paladin or the Maverick brothers – were just too hip."

"Two of my favorites were The Rifleman and Bonanza," F.K. added.

"In elementary school," noted J.D., "I watched

The Lone Ranger and Bonanza." Another Boomer remembered that she really liked Big Valley, and a male Boomer mentioned Wagon Train.

Animals played a big part on several westerns. For instance, Roy Rogers and Dale Evans had horses – Trigger and Buttermilk – and a dog, Bullet. And the Lone Ranger rode the trusty steed Silver, while his sidekick Tonto rode Scout.

Two horses – Fury and Mr. Ed – starred in their own shows. Is that cool, or what? And speaking of animals, Lassie and Rin-Tin-Tin headlined their own programs, too. "We watched Lassie and Fury and Sky King every Saturday morning, and loved them," P.M. recalled. "They made me cry because I was so afraid the horse, or the dog, or the people on Sky King's plane would be hurt, and would not be on the show anymore."

Sitcom classics

Not surprisingly, I Love Lucy rated at the top of the list for several Boomers. Today, over 50 years after the series premiered, Lucille Ball is still one of the most recognized faces on earth. "It was my favorite show through all those years, and through all the years since," said D.J. "I would still rather watch it instead of any regular show on television today."

"I watched That Girl – with Marlo Thomas – and M.A.S.H. My tastes became more in line with current cultural changes as I grew older," said J.D.

"M.A.S.H. was a perfect blend of some of the funniest dialog and some of the most poignant drama," remembered E.A. "It didn't show much of the violent aspects of the war. That part was implied or quickly shown, so that they could focus on the emotional aspects of the war and how humor was – and is – an excellent source of release in tense situations. I loved Klinger and Frank Burns for their humor."

"M.A.S.H. remains a classic," agreed A.T. "I watched reruns over and over with my Mom and Dad, and still find myself drawn in as I'm cruising through hundreds of cable channels."

"I liked the Adventures of Ozzie and Harriet," said R.S. "And Batman…what an escape from the reality of high school!"

"My favorite show for several years was Leave It To Beaver," an older Boomer recalled. "The classic character was Eddie Haskell, Wally's friend. I think most of us remember kids like that who were generally causing trouble, but acted super-polite around adults."

One Boomer said that "Father Knows Best seemed to capture what was ideal about 1950's America. It told the story of a happy middle-class family with three children living in a lovely town."

Commented T.C., a younger Boomer: "The Partridge family…I loved the music and the family dynamics."

Another younger Boomer, T.S. remembered "during elementary school, I enjoyed The Brady Bunch. I thought the older kids were so cool, and they got into the funniest situations."

Also getting positive mentions were My Three Sons, The Andy Griffith Show, Gilligan's Island, The Monkees, The Beverly Hillbillies, and Gomer Pyle, U.S.M.C.

A primetime weekly cartoon also got good ratings. "The Flintstones was on Friday night, my favorite night of the week," said R.H. Speaking of cartoons...several people voted for popular series like Crusader Rabbit, Mighty Mouse, Loony Tunes, and Felix the Cat.

Puppet series like Howdy Doody and Johnny Jupiter received votes, too, as did the television reruns of the old movie shorts The Three Stooges and The Little Rascals.

DID WINKY DINK START INTERACTIVE TELEVISION?

Today we know how to interact with a screen. We can order products, pay our bills, and even talk online to folks staring back at us.

But back in the 1950's and 1960's, that was just a dream. Then Winky Dink appeared.

He and his dog Woofer were cartoon characters created by Harry W. Prichett and Edwin Brit Wyckoff. Winky's adventures got him into lots of scrapes, but we kids could get him out. How?

We could order a little plastic sheet – sorta like sandwich wrap – we could place

on our TV screens. When Winky got into a jam, dots appeared on the screen. With our magic markers (as I remember, some sort of crayons), we drew on our screen to connect those dots to form a boat, a ladder, or whatever Winky needed to escape.

Another feature of the show was a "secret message" which Winky revealed. Again, we'd connect the dots to uncover that mystery.

For the first time, we could not only watch the action, but influence what might happen next. Is that interactive TV, or what?

Dramas and futuristic programs

The most frequently-mentioned program combining drama, the supernatural and futuristic fare was Rod Serling's classic Twilight Zone.

"My buddies would spend the night over at my house," said S.P. "We'd watch Twilight Zone, sneak out of the house, and get kind of creeped out walking around in the dark."

"During junior high and high school," T.S. said, "I remember I couldn't wait to get home to watch Dark Shadows. It was a spooky soap opera, and it had an element of being something I shouldn't watch because it was scary, along with a curiosity about the vampire life. I miss it!"

Said R.R.: "I think the original Twilight Zone series —

and maybe The Outer Limits – came along about the time I was in junior high school, and Star Trek began during my senior year. Star Trek in all its incarnations has stayed with me until this day as my first love.

"In college I always dashed home in time to see Dark Shadows…daytime soaps with a vampire touch!"

When it came to mysteries and detective series, Perry Mason, Highway Patrol, and Dragnet were remembered well. Noted S.W.: "As Joe Friday of Dragnet said, 'just the facts, ma'am.'"

M.F. remembered great mystery/detective shows, like "Route 66, 77 Sunset Strip, and Peter Gunn."

Other showed mentioned were Surfside Six, Hawaiian Eye, Bracken's World, The Defenders, Mannix, Mission Impossible, and Mod Squad.

Regarding medical dramas, our panelists voted for Ben Casey, Dr. Kildaire, and Marcus Welby, M.D.

The variety show

These shows of the 1950's and 1960's were perhaps the most popular on television. The one gathering the most votes in our survey was the Sunday evening Ed Sullivan Show.

"In junior high," said P.M., "our family would watch Ed Sullivan and Jackie Gleason along with Your Hit Parade and the start of American Bandstand. My siblings and I would laugh and dance and make believe we would one day be on television.

"My family all joined in on Sunday night for the next newest star introduced on Ed Sullivan. We had a black-and-white TV before I was ten years old, and the newspaper came out to our neighborhood and took our picture since we were the first ones on our block to get a TV. All the neighborhood kids came to watch it."

Formats for shows like Sullivan's included a great mix of current music, comedy, opera or Broadway tunes, perhaps puppets, a magic, juggling, or acrobatic act, maybe even a dramatic reading. And, Sullivan often introduced celebrities in the studio audience. Most of the acts were short, running about four to six minutes each.

"The show offered something for every family member, from children to old people," one Boomer marveled.

Over about 20 years – probably beginning with the Milton Berle show in the early 1950's – there were lots of programs like this. Two popular comedians – Jack Benny and Jackie Gleason – mixed comedy skits with variety acts.

Your Hit Parade and American Bandstand showcased contemporary music. Hit Parade – an evening show – featured four singers who alternated singing the week's top songs. The afternoon show American Bandstand presented music and performers that appealed to teens.

In the late 1960's, two upbeat variety platforms – Rowan and Martin's Laugh-In and The Smothers Brothers Comedy Hour – became especially popular with viewers.

Mickey Mouse Club

Perhaps the most popular afternoon show for Boomers was The Mickey Mouse Club. It originally aired for the first time in 1955–1959, and was revived with different casts in the 1970's and 1990's.

"My favorite TV show, for sure, was The Mickey Mouse Club," said A.M. The show offered comedy, music, cartoons, a newsreel, and kids with special talents.

Each day of the week had a different theme. "I liked Wednesday," S.W. remembered, "which was 'Anything Can Happen Day.'" Monday offered fun with music. Tuesday featured a guest star. Thursday was circus day, and Friday presented a talent round-up.

During the program, several action adventure serials aired. Two I remember well were "Spin and Marty," about two boys at a summer camp, and the "Hardy Boys" mystery series.

Davy Crockett

Before the Partridge Family, before the Beatles, even before Elvis, a heroic frontiersman – actually, the actor who portrayed him – set off a nationwide frenzy.

In 1954, the hit ABC TV series Walt Disney's Wonderful World of Color began a three-part drama series based on pioneer Davy Crockett's life. All three episodes – including the one where he died at the Alamo – had been filmed before the first one aired.

But about 40 million people saw that first episode, loved it, and began to buy just about any merchandise connected with Crockett. This included fringed shirts, coonskin frontier caps, guitars, and much more. Within the first year, about $300 million in Crockett goods had been sold.

The series became so phenomenally successful that the studio made two more episodes about Crockett's earlier exploits: Davy Crockett's Keelboat Race and Davy Crockett and the River Pirates.

There's also a frontier postscript to this story: From 1964 to 1970 Fess Parker – who'd played Crockett in the Disney series – starred as Daniel Boone on another TV series.

Source for Crockett material: Newsweek feature November 13, 2006 by Marc Peyser.

DID OUR TV SHOWS TEACH VALUES?

Television in the 1950's and 1960's was far different from the formats we watch today. The weekday shows most of my friends remember were situation comedies. During the weekends – especially on Saturday mornings – the entertainment was mostly action/adventure fare.

A significant part of Baby Boomer television was a "values" component. The comedies often communicated a lesson about honesty, integrity, or treating others with respect. The main character often learned something.

Let's look at a few of these shows – both comedies and dramas – and examine their themes:

1. Gunsmoke – This western featured U.S. Marshal Matt Dillon and deputy Chester, along with an attractive lady saloon owner and Dodge City's physician. One of the best-written shows in the history of the medium, it began in the 1950's and continues today in reruns. The main characters were highly motivated, and tried their best to protect their community from some really bad guys.

2. The Real McCoys – Walter Brennan as Grandpa Amos headed this sitcom about a multi-generational California farming family. Grandpa often passed family values and lore along, but occasionally learned something useful from the young folks, too.

3. Father Knows Best – This comedy about a middle-class American family featured Robert Young as the father and Jane Wyatt as the mother. Their three children Betty, Bud, and Kathy frolicked through age-appropriate school adventures. Some people believe this show excelled at depicting life and values in the 1950's.

4. The Jack Benny Show and The Red Skelton Show – These variety programs – led by two of the world's finest stage comedians – offered both skit comedy and guest stars. It's reported that several Baby Boomer actors say they were especially influenced by Jack Benny's sketches, where Jack often played the guy feeding straight lines to others who would reply with a joke.

5. Annie Oakley – This Saturday morning western star, along with Dale Evans in the Roy Rogers Show, presented ladies as powerful heroes. It was one of the first TV programs to show women in leadership roles.

These are only a few of the shows which communicated American societal values to youngsters.

So...what points did these five shows share? They reminded viewers that (a) good triumphs over evil, (b) clean comedy can be very funny, (c) most Americans in the 1950's and 1960's considered themselves "middle class," (d) every generation's got something to share with those who came before and after it, and (e) both genders can become leaders.

Top television during two pivotal years

We want to give you a brief look at the top shows that ran during the middle years of both the 1950's and 1960's. Here they are:

<u>1955–1956</u>
1. The $64,000 Question – game show
2. I Love Lucy – comedy
3. The Ed Sullivan Show – variety
4. Disneyland – adventure/variety
5. The Jack Benny Show – comedy/variety
6. December Bride – comedy
7. You Bet Your Life – game show
8. Dragnet – drama/adventure
9. The Millionaire – drama
10. I've Got A Secret – game show
Source: FiftiesWeb.com

<u>1965–1966</u>
1. Bonanza – western
2. Gomer Pyle, U.S.M.C. – comedy
3. The Lucy Show – comedy
4. The Red Skelton Hour – variety
5. Batman (Thursday) – comedy/adventure
6. The Andy Griffith Show – comedy
7. Bewitched – comedy
8. The Beverly Hillbillies – comedy
9. Hogan's Heroes – comedy
10. Batman (Wednesday) – comedy/adventure
Source: FiftiesWeb.com

What did we learn?

1. Our television choices were mostly limited to three networks and a few independent stations.

2. We because the first generation to be raised in television households. This profoundly influenced how we learn and assimilate information.

3. Western dramas became a big part of our television diet. In most of these, the heroes and villains were immediately identifiable. This may have led to how we perceived the world as we grew older.

4. I Love Lucy is a huge favorite among Boomers. Most of the sitcoms preferred by our panel featured traditional white middle-class families in traditional contemporary situations.

5. Because of reruns, our children grew up watching and learning from many of the same shows we did. This gives us a unique link to the next generation.

6. Animated shows were popular in our childhood, and remain so today.

7. The Twilight Zone was the most-preferred supernatural or futuristic show, followed closely by the daytime drama Dark Shadows. Perhaps our fascination with this genre was fueled by 1950's and 1960's emphasis on the space race and exploring worlds beyond our own.

8. Courtroom, police, and private detective dramas have remained a major feature on TV for nearly 50 years. Does this emphasize our belief in law and ultimate justice?

9. Variety shows dominated prime-time television during our childhood, but few exist today. Why? Some speculate that previous generations attended vaudeville-type stage show, so they were comfortable with short stage acts, and a variety format. We seem to favor theme formats (comedy clubs, rock shows, band reunion tours, stage plays, etc.).

10. The Mickey Mouse Club was a unique American institution. The daytime series was so popular it was revived in two later decades. It showcased moral values, children, remarkable youth talent, and valuable information packaged in a format virtually everyone enjoyed.

11. The Davy Crockett adventures captured public attention, and led to one of the first and largest merchandising events in the nation's history.

12. TV hit shows of the mid-1950's reveal the public loved variety and game shows.

13. Television shows ten years later – in 1965 – featured mostly situation comedy.

CHAPTER 17
Most memorable day
of a Boomer's life?

There's no surprise about the day Boomers remember most often. By a wide margin, it's November 22, 1963, the day John F. Kennedy died. Not only do Boomers remember it, they remember where they were and what they were doing.

And some recall the exact feelings that had when they first heard the news. "I still remember which school room I was in," R.S. said. "It was an annex, a temporary building."

But his feelings weren't temporary. They're permanent, etched in his memory.

Likewise, most Boomers vividly recount what they saw on their televisions July 20, 1969. That's the day American astronaut Neil Armstrong set foot on the moon, and made "one small step for man, one giant leap for mankind."

After reliving those two eventful days, Boomers in our focus group replied with answers as varied and complex as the individuals themselves.

The space race

"I'll always remember March 6, 1961, when Alan Shepard became the first American in space...even if briefly," said K.H. America's efforts to launch a man into space – and later to put astronauts in orbit – captured every citizen's attention.

The country's initial space program – Project Mercury – lasted from 1959 to 1963, and included the missions of seven military test pilots.

Several Boomers emphasized that John Glenn – the third American into space and the first to orbit this planet – was one of their heroes.

Among younger Boomers, "The Challenger disaster (in 1986) is the event that first comes to mind," said T.C.

'Meeting' the Beatles

"I remember staying at a friend's house for a slumber party in an upstairs playroom," says E.A. "The Beatles premiered that night on the Ed Sullivan Show, singing 'I want to hold your hand.' You'll have to look up the year." (I did. It was 1964.)

"It may not have been the most significant event, but certainly memorable," she added.

What made this event more notable was not only the Beatles' enormous talent, but the niche they created as new heroes to youngsters. "John F. Kennedy was the first 'young' President," said D.C., "and seemed to represent the Boomers because of his youth." When Kennedy died, some say, teens had no major heroes until they heard those joyful Beatle beats.

Thinking about the Wall

"Without a doubt," said J.D. firmly, "I remember waking up every morning and hearing accounts of how many people had tried to escape over the Berlin Wall, how many had made it, and how many had been killed.

"It made me realize that not everyone had the same freedoms that I did. Later, the events become even more significant when I taught with a woman who had lost her foot fleeing East Germany."

Visions of Vietnam

Many Boomers – both older and younger – stressed that the Vietnam era produced lasting, haunting memories. For the early Boomers – especially the guys – that's understandable.

These boys came of age during the time of a military draft. At the age of 18, each male registered with the Selective Service System. He could be called up and asked to report to training camp at any time, provided he did NOT have a deferment or exemption.

Regarding military deferments: most common was the 2-S. This identified a person as a full-time student in a high school or college.

"The most significant event of my life," said an older Boomer, "came in November 1971, the day I was formally discharged from the Army."

Younger Boomers, however, did not have to deal with the draft. They could choose the military as a career option, but were not required to serve.

"I guess Vietnam was the most important event historically," said E.A., "but I was much more wrapped up in school talent shows and dances and boys."

"When I was in 10th grade," R.R., recalls, "I remember hearing on the radio one morning that a member of the U.S. peace-keeping force had been killed in Vietnam. Whether that was the beginning or not, it was the first time Vietnam truly entered my awareness."

"I remember watching former prisoners of war coming home and getting off the plane, possibly in 1970 or 1971," noted G.M. "It made quite an impression on me."

"The end of the Vietnam War," said A.T., a younger Boomer, "was a major event for me, although I was really too young to understand the significance of the soldiers returning home."

Tragedies remembered

Personal tragedies, of course, made the biggest impressions. "When I was four, my father died," said D.J. "That was certainly a life-changing event."

Not surprisingly, many sad public events of our youth stayed with us. "I remember being a Southerner, integration, and watching the work of Martin Luther King," said P.D.

"Our innocence was taken away," R.R. responds sadly. "JFK was assassinated. That was followed by the deaths of Robert Kennedy and Martin Luther King.

"It seemed for a while that everything was going from bad to worse," she continued. "It seemed the world was going mad."

"The shootings at Kent State horrified me," said G.M.

"Who could forget the Watergate conspiracy?" added D.S.

On the plus side, two Boomers recalled positive national and personal events.

"I'll never forget the day Hank Aaron beat Babe Ruth's career home run record," said T.S.

"Leaving for college in September of 1968 was a huge event for me," recalled J.H.

What did we learn?

1. Profound personal and national tragedies made lasting impressions on us. These impressions seared our memories, and were reinforced by visual televised images.

2. Music of the 1960's and 1970's allowed us to express shared conflicted feelings of both anxiety and hope. (Notable examples: the songs "Eve of Destruction" and "Age of Aquarius.")

3. A large percentage of us saw John F. Kennedy as the personification of a Youth Movement in America. His death shattered us, reminding us that life is both precious and unpredictable.

4. The Berlin Wall showed Americans that we enjoyed freedoms and economic prosperity shared by few other societies.

5. Feelings about Vietnam and its aftermath are still unclear. Was it a war against Communism or simply a country's civil war? What did we gain – or lose – by participation in it?

6. Many early male Boomers – in an effort to delay military service – stayed in school to receive additional education and even advanced degrees. Learning literally became a life-saver for some.

7. The tragic deaths of several young leaders – JFK, Robert Kennedy, Martin Luther King, John

Lennon – convinced us that life could be short, and that we must live for today. "Carpe diem" – seize the day – became a frequently-heard slogan.

8. Shootings on a college campus, plus student/police riots during the 1968 Democratic Convention and the Watergate conspiracy, made us re-examine our reliance on authority figures.

CHAPTER 18
Who had the greatest influence on us?

By a comfortably wide margin, our Boomer panel voted "Mom" as the person who most influenced their lives.

"I saw in her qualities that I longed to have...her patience, her choice to take the high road, her self-sacrifice," one person replied. "Not everyone would admire self-sacrifice, but it was an honorable quality, even if it meant she was less happy than she might otherwise have been.

"She sacrificed herself for the sake of her children. Also, I rarely heard her say a bad thing about anyone.

"Now, when I struggle with how to react to some life event, I find myself wondering how Mom would have dealt with it."

"I was an only child," said J.D., "and my Dad died when I was seven. Mom was of course the biggest influence."

"My mother," commented M.F., "has shown me how to take life as it is, and not be fearful...at least most of the time!"

"My mother taught me I could do anything," said K.L., "and the only true failure is a failure to try. She also taught me to laugh."

One grandmother received a great compliment. "I was blessed to be raised in a Christian home," remembered F.K. "However, the matriarch of that legacy was my mother's mother. My grandmother has been the single greatest positive influence on my life.

"Of course my father and mother come in at position number 1.2! My grandmother's faith – she walked the talk – was foremost, and for that I am eternally grateful."

Dad and parents

Said R.H.: "My father influenced me most. He has more character and integrity than anyone I have met in my entire life. He remains my hero and ultimate role model."

"I suppose my Dad had the greatest influence in my life culturally and professionally," another older Boomer – now a physician – emphasized. "I liked the respect he received from his friends and patients, and I could tell it was mutual."

"My parents acting as a team influenced me," said R.R. "I received my mother's love of life, her soft heart, her affection for music and literature. I received my father's attention to detail and his sense of old-world formality.

"They gave me the tools with which to walk through this life by educating me in everything from the Bible to simple good manners and compassion."

"My dad taught me to be as independent as I could safely be," said S.W. "My mom taught me that there is a spiritual world we mere humans cannot see."

Other influential people

"My wife has influenced me most," said D.C. "For 35 years, she continues to support what I do, and helps me get over the bumps in the road. She is the perfect complement to me, and together we have grown more than we ever would have.

"The influence she has had is one of thoughtfulness, level thinking, smart humor, and great counsel. She tempers my enthusiasm with a sense of reality that is often needed."

"I have loved being married to the man I am married to," said H.J. "I was not really a shy, meek, or mild child, but my husband is strong-willed and very outspoken. In order to get into his life, I had to become so much stronger emotionally. He made me wake up each day and face whatever I was going to do, whether it was go to work, take care of kids, or be a leader in any organization I belonged to. I feel like I am a very happy, optimistic person because of him."

"My children," emphasized R.S. "The quote is 'the son is the father to the man,' and it made sense to me when I realized that my children had taught me the most important things in life."

"My uncle," said D.J., "was the only man in my family, and he was the first to treat me like an adult."

"My brother," said a younger Boomer. "We are so much alike in so many ways, and completely opposite in others. He is fearless, utterly independent, an entrepreneur and a risk-taker. I am none of those things.

"But I think the traits that make him so comfortable forging new paths for himself also make him slow to connect with people, and make him not able, or perhaps not interested, in making and sustaining friendships. I think I'm a better friend, co-worker, etc. because of my ability to empathize, to understand others' feelings, motivations, needs, and weaknesses."

"My cousin," said J.D., "is 87 years old, lives in California, has traveled all over the world, and is the most stimulating, challenging person I know."

National figures

On a national scale, one Boomer said he was influenced by "Bill Gates. Without the company he created, I would not have some of the opportunities I have today."

Another older Boomer admired "Winston Churchill, because he was so robust and dramatic, and loyal to the ideals of the British Empire."

What did we learn?

1. The ones closest to us – mostly those who lived in our household – influenced us the most.

2. The people who influenced us the most are the ones who taught us the most.

3. Spouses and children have a powerful influence on our motivations and decisions.

4. People who influenced us the most often also helped us decide on career paths.

5. National leaders can influence us by how they define goals and set examples.

Chapter 19
Comments and compliments that made big impressions

Sometimes a teacher's or friend's comment can alter a person's life. We asked our panel what positive – or life-changing – comments they'd always remember.

"This wasn't a spoken comment," recalled T.S. "My 7th grade English teacher appointed me her back-up grader for quizzes. So, after a quiz, some students would take their papers to the teacher and, if she was busy grading a paper, students could bring their papers to me to grade them. I was honored and flattered. It was a real show of confidence."

"When I won the American Legion award in 6th grade," D.S. said, "my teacher said I was loyal, honest, hard-working, and a great role model to the school."

"In 10th grade I got my head buzz cut as all the basketball team did in an era of long hair," remembered D.C. "My English teacher made an issue of how good my haircut was compared to the 'longhairs.'"

"My teacher," recalled K.L., "said that I could be anything I wanted to be."

"Happy graduation," laughed one older Boomer, today a radio show host. "Actually, what the teacher said was more like 'He certainly never runs out of things to say. I used that as career motivation."

"The greatest thing a teacher did for me came in 7th grade," D.L. said. "I said something to another guy, and he attacked me after class. The teacher broke up the fight, and sent the other guy to the principal. The next day we fought again, and again I took the silver medal.

"I don't know what she did, but I never saw him again. She had moved him to another side of the school."

Laments R.W. : "I was a scared little mouse in elementary and junior high school. I never held my hand up in class, always tried to be just plain invisible. I do have one vague memory of someone, most likely a teacher, telling me how well I could spell. I have loved words ever since."

"My home economics teacher was very nurturing," P.M. recalled fondly. "She knew I needed some self-confidence before I went to college, and she was so good at keeping my spirits up."

"I have the feeling there was positive feedback all the time," said R.S. "Maybe one thing was when the jazz band director acknowledged my contribution by switching from a popular instrument to one for which we had trouble finding players."

More life-altering phrases

"I was a decent student," said A.T., "solid A-B grades with little or no effort. I'm sure my teachers thought and spoke well of me, but I can't remember anything specific any of them said to me.

"However, I recall well when my guidance counselor – in my senior year of high school – made arrangements for me to speak with the Princeton representative visiting campus. It felt good that I was the only student called in front of my classmates to meet with the Princeton rep."

"One of my dear friends," a younger Boomer commented, "said to me that good people are attracted to other good people. Her simple words made me completely re-evaluate my role in my friendships, and really my role in the world. Eight simple words made me realize that I am one of the good guys."

D.S. shared a mid-life comment: "After I'd been raising a family, and out of the work force for 25 years, a friend convinced me that my volunteer experience was valuable and would translate into a paying job. I took the chance and applied for jobs, and was pleased to find several employers appreciated the volunteer experience."

Unusual or negative advice

"My friend told me all the boys in Mexico loved blond American girls, so I went to a school in Mexico the summer after my sophomore year to test the validity of her statement," said one Boomer.

"She was right, but that's not what changed my life. I realized I had a gift for mimicking sounds and learning Spanish. I have now taught Spanish for 36 years and traveled extensively in Latin America and Spain. So my friend really pointed me toward a career."

> **"In the 10th grade,"** said an older Boomer, **"the counselor in my high school looked at my grades, and the fact that I was poor, and informed me I should take distributive education. The comment: 'You need to learn some sort of trade to support yourself until you get married.' It never entered my mind to ask why, or to go to college."**

"I had several teachers in high school who took extra time to give individual guidance, which I still remember today," another older Boomer recalled. "But the most decisive was the day in senior year that my father – who tended never to give specific advice, only encouraging us to decide for ourselves – said it would be a bad idea to go into music as a profession."

"My basketball coach," laughed R.H., "said to me during tryouts: 'Son, you can't shoot, but you sure are slow.' It was then I realized my dreams of a professional athletic career were probably not realistic, and I turned to broadcasting."

"This wasn't a comment," a younger Boomer laughed, "but it positively affected my life. My teacher and my Mom found out I was giving a friend one Pop Tart if he did my long division. I had two tarts each day, so that was a pretty good trade.

"Then one day, out of the blue, Mom removed one of the tarts from the package. After two days with no Pop Tarts I learned to do my own long division. That was a life-changer."

What did we learn?

1. Sometimes the most positive messages from teachers were unspoken. This included giving a student an extra assignment or job that reflected the teacher's trust and approval.

2. Classroom and school awards gave Boomers positive feedback, and many are still remembered.

3. Sometimes an instructor may be the first to notice a special talent or skill on which a person can build a career.

4. Occasionally the most positive effect a teacher can have on a student is to serve as an interested listener.

5. Teachers are often the first to discover, and reinforce, one's ability to act as a team player.

6. A positive referral from a teacher can profoundly affect a student's attitude and career choice.

7. Friends who know us well can often point us in new and positive directions.

8. Negative comments can be life-changing. Negative comments can also affect career options.

Chapter 20
The question people asked us most: "What do you want to be when you grow up?"

Teachers used to ask me this all the time. How about you?

Times have changed considerably since the 1960's and 1970's. Women's and men's roles have been altered and redefined.

The ladies speak

My wife – who became an English teacher – remembers talking with her parents about four traditional "female" alternatives: teacher, nurse, flight attendant, and – since she had learned foreign languages – an interpreter at the United Nations.

One Boomer said she originally aspired to several of the careers just mentioned. "I fell into a delightful set of books about a nurse named Cherry Ames," she reminisced. "I just knew what I wanted to be when I grew up. I really wanted to be a nurse...until I watched my Dad gut and scale the newest catch of perch on the back steps. That pretty much did it for my nursing career.

"Then I fell head over heels with the idea of being an airline stewardess, as it was called in those days. But

I never grew over the minimum height of 5'2". I still love airports and aviation to this day.

"After that, I thought it would be interesting to learn different languages and work as an interpreter at the U.N., or perhaps work in an American embassy abroad. However, when it came down to actually learning the languages, I realized I was doing good to master my own Texas language...and that was that."

"I wanted to be a flight attendant," recalled D.S., "because it meant traveling to exotic places which I had never done. I had never flown in an airplane."

"I wanted to get married and be a mom," said E.A.

"A movie star!" exclaimed M.F. "Go figure...me the tomboy! I always wished that people would say I looked like Marilyn Monroe. But almost everyone who said 'You look like...' would end the sentence with 'Hayley Mills.'"

"When I was in 6th grade," P.M. related, "the school gave polio shots in the nurse's office to all the kids. The doctor asked for a volunteer to wipe the student's arm down with alcohol, and then he administered the shot. I volunteered, and loved doing it, and just knew I would be a nurse. As I got older, I changed my mind on that."

"I wanted to be a writer," said T.C., "because using words was something I was good at. Of course, I had no understanding of writing except as a fiction writer, which seemed like a whole lot of work. When I discovered journalism in high school, it was a great revelation! I could write every day and get paid for it."

Said K.L.: "I wanted to be a Broadway actress, singing and dancing. Why? Because I was in elementary school, and had no clue."

A.T. had a slightly different dream. "I wanted to be a marine biologist, even though I was from a land-locked region. I loved to swim and loved the beach, and thought marine biology was the next best thing to being a mermaid."

"Believe it or not," M.H. noted, "I wanted to write songs. I actually wrote two in elementary school, and the teacher taught them to the class. Was I ever hot stuff!"

"I wanted to be a detective," J.D. told us, "because I loved Nancy Drew books."

What about the guys?

This writer – a skinny, weak city boy – wanted to be either a cowboy, Superman, or a professional athlete. I realized by age nine that none of these were viable options.

D.L. said he wanted to be "a soldier or FBI man. I was patriotic, and loved watching John Wayne war movies with my Dad. Playing for the Dallas Cowboys was ruled out because I sensed I needed athletic ability and size."

"I wanted to be a pro football quarterback," said R. L. "Why? Because the good-looking girls loved the quarterback."

D.C. cast another vote for sports, as a "pro basketball player."

"I honestly don't remember," said R.S. "But I had a big interest in music, and had a dream of leading a jazz band."

P.B., a successful inventor, said his early hobby led to his future profession. "I always liked to make stuff. Guess I just never stopped."

"I didn't have a clue what I wanted to do then," laughed D.J., "and I don't now, either."

Upwardly mobile?

No matter what we wanted to be at age ten, huge numbers of us sensed we needed education...and lots of it.

A study by the U.S. Census Bureau found that "The proportion of Americans with at least a bachelors' degree grew five-fold from 1950 to 2003, from 3.4% to 17.4%. The percentage completing high school quadrupled from 1950 to 2003, from 17% to 71.5%."

Boomers, who grew up in a time of emerging prosperity, were apparently convinced that more education led to more opportunity.

What did we learn?

1. In their early years, many Boomer women felt that job choices were limited. After education and additional training, they've moved into a multitude of careers which were traditionally considered men's jobs.

2. During pre-teen years, many Boomers considered high-profile careers in professional sports or entertainment. Boomers were the first generation whose

childhoods centered around television, where they constantly saw sports and entertainment programs.

3. Several people told us that – even in their middle years – career change is still possible and, in some cases, probable.

Chapter 21
Over 50,000 people Baby Boomers admire

When we Boomers shop for someone to admire, we've got choices galore. Never in the history of humankind have there been more media targeting us with messages about so many.

That's why we've listed a few of them below in alphabetical order. If we Boomers know one thing, it's the alphabet. (What many of us can't remember, however, is that poem about "I before e, except after c." Or is it the other way around?)

Anyway, some of the names cited belong to our own generation. Others made a great impression on us. "I guess I am prone to admire people older than I," said one respondent. Most of the people selected by our focus group are still alive today.

One other note: Several Boomers praised individuals who are NOT in the public eye. To preserve their privacy, their names are not listed.

American Veterans -- "50,000-plus men and women who gave their lives in Vietnam. We also honor the men and women who were mistreated on their return to the United States," a Boomer wrote.

Angelou, Maya – This author, historian, and poet is a role model to many.

Beatles – John, Paul, George, and Ringo retain their popularity.

Berners-Lee, Tim – Invented the World Wide Web in 1989.

Bono – "Like his music or not, he seems to be able to transcend politics to achieve good things for the most needy on our planet," said M.F. "He's a rock star with a conscience," another Boomer emphasized.

Brokaw, Tom – Anchor of NBC News for many years.

Bush, George W. – Several expressed admiration for the 43rd U.S. President.

Clinton, Bill – The former President received several votes "for his continuing contributions to the world as well as his service to the country," said R.S.

Clinton, Hillary – "Willing to be a wife and mother, but doesn't see her gender as an impediment to having an impact," said T.C.

Diana, Princess – "Not just a pretty face, but a caring woman who wanted to use her position to make a difference," said one respondent.

Dylan, Bob – This musician spoke for anti-war and anti-establishment causes, said one Boomer. He was a major figure in 1960's folk music.

Gates, Bill – He got more votes than anyone, and was recognized for major contributions to technology, philosophy, and education. He and his associates have "brought about so much technology with the computer industry that most of us could not get along without them," said P.M. He has "brought the world closer together, and exposed areas of basic human need," said A.T.

Gates, Melinda – Philanthropy. She and her husband Bill "focus on global problems not adequately addressed by governments and non-profits," a member of our focus group said.

Glenn, John – The former astronaut and U.S. Senator "seemed to always represent the correct morals, patriotism and ethics to become a role model for most of our generation," emphasized D.C.

Gore, Al – The former Vice-President and later Presidential candidate shows "persistence in fighting to bring environmental issues to the awareness of many," said L.A. Another Boomer emphasized that he is "always on the cutting edge, a harbinger of things to come." He has "worked to educate the world on the dangers of global warming, and what we can do to be less energy-dependent," added D.S.

Hoffman, Dustin – This actor starred in "The Graduate," one of our generation's most popular movies.

Jobim, Antonio Carlos – "He invented a music fit for a whole word," said D.J.

Jobs, Steve – Co-founder of Apple, and a major figure in computer and technology industries.

Kennedy, John – He's often cited as the first hero of Baby Boomers.

Kennedy, Robert – JFK's younger brother, and Presidential candidate himself, is admired for his inspirational messages and focus on the poor.

King, Martin Luther – Civil rights leader, minister, author. Many have called him "the outstanding speaker of the second half of the 21st century."

Koppel, Ted – Long-time host of the ABC "Nightline" program.

Limbaugh, Rush – Radio commentator and talk show host.

Ma, Yo Yo – The famous cellist was named "for bringing incredible beauty to the world."

Marsalis, Winton – The composer and trumpeter is recognized "for revitalizing jazz in the United States," said R.S.

McCain, John – Decorated Vietnam veteran, prisoner-of-war, U.S. Senator, Presidential candidate.

McCartney, Paul – Wrote music and songs promoting love and peace.

Reagan, Ronald – This former President and great communicator is a role model to many.

Ripkin, Cal – Viewed as a gentleman and athlete, he's seen as a role model to both his own and later generations.

Royal, Darrell – This legendary University of Texas football coach "did his best, did it with dignity and ethics, and knew when he was done," said an admirer.

Russert, Tim – The host of "Meet the Press" was named for "his honest attempt to bring truth to journalism, and for his humble devotion to his heritage," said J.D.

Spielberg, Steven – Award-winning American director and producer.

Staubach, Roger – He is a "Naval Academy graduate, Heisman Trophy winner, former quarterback of the Dallas Cowboys, Vietnam veteran, Christian, great businessman, and just an all-around outstanding role model," said D.L.

Swink, Dr. Jim – This former All-American running back from TCU – and later orthopedic surgeon -- made a great impression on one Boomer, who added that he "took time for some kids when he didn't have to, and was a bigger-than-life hero in every sense. He spoiled me for all time."

Winfrey, Oprah – The noted talk show host is "the epitome of the American success story," and recognized for "humanitarian efforts," said B.C. "She provides fundamental and essential wisdom and grace to the human experience, (and) empowers people – especially women – to live lives that fulfill them," added another. She has "used her wealth and fame to help others," D.S. emphasized.

Wonder, Stevie – This brilliant composer creates upbeat, inspiring songs, and has sought to overcome racial barriers.

What did we learn?

1. People Baby Boomers most admire (10) come more frequently from the field of politics than any other.

2. The next groups of people Boomers most admire come from music (7) or media (7) professions.

3. Although we suggested in our questionnaire that Boomers select outstanding members of their own generation, many selected people who were slightly older.

4. It appears there is some correlation between the celebrities we most admire and the ones we've seen longest. Many celebrities mentioned have made important contributions to society over many years.

Some have been on the world stage for decades.

5. The power of television, radio, and the internet has made celebrities virtual "visitors in our homes." This makes us feel we share a special kinship with them.

6. Does "absence make the heart grow fonder?" Based on our research, we conclude the exact opposite.

CHAPTER 22
What famous people would you like to meet, or invite for dinner?

Folks in the public eye – building their own careers – often help us define ourselves. How? By comparing our social or political beliefs with theirs, we can better sort out our personal feelings.

Unfortunately, several people we would like to meet lived in prior generations, or even in ancient history. So we asked focus group members to tell us (1) what famous people made an impression on them, and (2) what four historical characters they'd invite to dinner.

Contemporaries

"Billy Graham has been a Christian counselor to our Presidents for over 50 years. What stories he could tell," emphasized R.R.

One lady talked about how "Being raised a Catholic, I think Mother Teresa would have been interesting to talk to, especially how she related to her God."

Said J.D.:"I would like to talk to Chuck Yeager, and ask how he could be so brave."

"I have read his book and seen his show," said P.M., "and really related to Bill Cosby as a person and parent. I don't care about politics or entertainers or people in the public arena, so I loved Cosby's stories and I could relate to what he talked about.

"I would also like to invite Laura Bush – or maybe just any First Lady – who has watched her husband be President of the United States. I would like to know what they talk about at the dinner table, how much time the President has had to be part of his girls' lives, and how she has remained such a beautiful First Lady inside and out. But I would like to know that about a lot of First Ladies. It is a hard life."

"Jim Wright," said a Texas Boomer, "taught me more about how to govern than any professor."

"I would invite Robin Williams, who is the funniest person in history," said D.C.

"Two of my guests would be Darrell Royal, the great University of Texas coach, and singer Norah Jones," said D.J.

And speaking of singers, another Boomer said "Louis Armstrong and Tony Bennett love what they do, and it radiates. If you don't love what you're doing…get out of the business! These guys made – or make – us smile whenever we see them."

Recent past

John and Jacqueline Kennedy received a number of votes. "They captivated my imagination when I was young," said R.T. "That would be some lively dinner conversation, don't you think?"

"JFK would be one of the people I most respect," added S.W. "Also, Martin Luther King would fit into that category, as would Mahatma Gandhi."

"Franklin Roosevelt," emphasized J.D., "overcame a handicap to become one of our greatest Presidents."

Both Franklin and Eleanor Roosevelt were cited by some Boomers, who wanted to know more about their lives and how they worked together. "I would like to hear his reflections on managing World War II, and especially what he would do differently in hindsight," said a respondent.

From that same era, one Boomer wanted his dinner companions to be Winston Churchill, Douglas MacArthur, and golf great Bobby Jones.

"Bertrand Russell," said R.S., "had a big impact on my life at one point. For me, he was like Einstein is for most people. I could understand the mathematical challenges he tackled at the beginning of his career, as well as his broad interest in social issues."

"Princess Diana made a great impression on me," said T.R. "She was such a lovely and giving person who rose above such adverse circumstances to be her own person. When all the specials aired on the tenth anniversary of her death, I was still moved to tears. I would love to see what else she would have done with her life."

"Last year," P.M. remembered, "our girls took us to Yankee Stadium for a baseball game, and there was so much of Babe Ruth around that it was someone you would love to have known. He would have been interesting to talk to. Our family loved baseball, even though we had only girls, but we spent a lot of time going to games as a family. To have known someone like the Babe would have made for interesting conversation."

"Richard P. Feynman is my favorite physicist," said A.T. "Not that I ever studied physics, but Feynman had such broad appeal. He was the youngest scientist to participate in the atomic research at Los Alamos. Toward the end of this life, he made physics accessible to everyone by serving on the Presidential Commission investigating the explosion of the space shuttle Challenger.

"It was Feynman who picked up the rubber o-ring, plunged it into a glass of ice water, and demonstrated that the cold made the rubber ring less pliable and more prone to fuel leaks. He won the Nobel Prize, and was a recorded bongo player!"

For her dinner guests, K.L. chose "Winston Churchill for his biting wit and conviction; Picasso for his talent; Nelly Bly for her daring and sense of adventure; and Barbara Jordan...just to listen to her voice as she tells political stories and discusses current events."

"Bob Hope was a great comedian who never got his material from the gutter," said F.K. "I especially admire his dedication to the U.S. Armed Forces."

Other potential dinner guests nominated included pilot Amelia Earhart and baseball great Mickey Mantle.

Nineteenth century and before

We've listed these historical figures alphabetically, and added comments when they were made by focus group members:

Dante Alighieri – "He had an imagination – and he was such a poet – to put it all into an allegory which would last forever, and which would be the basis for the western concept of Heaven and Hell for hundreds of years. Where did he get all that?"

Susan B. Anthony

Simone de Beauvier

Elizabeth I – "Such a fascinating woman and politician...really a politically astute figure."

F. Scott Fitzgerald

Benjamin Franklin

Thomas Jefferson

Jesus – "I would ask him how passive an example we should try to be, if passive at all." Another comment: "If He was here, He could personally tell me what He would do."

Leonardo da Vinci – "What a mind he had!"

Abraham Lincoln

Kate Millet

Francois Rabelais – "He was the bon vivant of the Renaissance. He felt that there was always something on the other side of tragedy to make us rejoice in life. He was – like his character Gargantua – bigger than life. His philosophy: we can either laugh or cry, and he chose to laugh. His portrait is hanging in my dining room!"

Robert the Bruce – "I'd ask him if he had any regrets, and what they would be."

Henry David Thoreau – "He's someone I return to over and over again. For someone with a relatively narrow life experience, he saw a much wider world. He expressed clearly and simply basic tenets for living a complete life. I like what he had to say, and how he said it."

Mark Twain – "He was funny and sharp, and presented the world he lived in with a twinkle in his eye." Another Boomer's comment: "I would just love to sit and hear him talk about anything."

William Wallace – "He inspired his contemporaries to find and win their freedom. Today – after seven centuries – his memory lives on in literature and film to hopefully inspire future generations to fight against tyranny and for freedom."

George Washington
Virginia Woolf

What did we learn?

1. We are interested in religious leaders and advisors, and feel we can benefit from their philosophies.

2. The largest category of famous people mentioned were involved in politics and government.

3. We expressed an interest in sports figures, perhaps because we view so many sports on television.

4. Three great minds of science – Leonardo da Vinci, Bertrand Russell, and Richard P. Feynman – were mentioned by our panel. We admire those whose philosophical and technical abilities have advanced society.

5. The large number of writers mentioned indicates we value literary pursuits and the history of our society.

Chapter 23
How should we prepare to face the future?

It's funny how goals change from one year to the next. When we're kids, the goal seems always to be about TOMORROW. "Tomorrow I'll start first grade," or "Tomorrow it'll be Halloween," or "Tomorrow we'll go visit Grandma."

But as years move forward, we learn from experience. We begin to prioritize, dividing goals into short-term and long-term. A short-term goal, for instance, might be to do well on a test...the long-term goal is to graduate.

As we transition from school to career, marriage, and family planning, our goals intermingle. Should we take a better job if takes us away from our fiance' or spouse, or from a growing family?

If you're a Boomer, you've already answered these questions. If you're younger, you may be facing them now.

We middle-agers have learned that planning for the future may require occasional readjustments.

Short-term

"While abstract," said one respondent, "one goal would be to achieve and maintain peace in my life.

I hate conflict, and…it makes me see how important it is just to live a peaceful live. I strive for peace on a daily basis.

"And, I want to have fun and be nice to myself. I would like to do something fun every single day. I have set up a system of weekly rewards that I really look forward to."

A sports-minded Boomer emphasized that "I'd like to go to the Masters again, and to Fenway Park. Those are icon-like places for a sports enthusiast. And I'd like to have a single-digit golf handicap when I retire. I want to overcome years of bad swings."

Contemplates R.R.: "I want to see Italy, Scotland, and Ireland to visit the land of my ancestors. There's so much beauty to behold…and besides, why let the travel writers have all the fun?"

"I'd like to pay off two rent houses, live a healthy, active life, and be happy. These are my goals because they are simple and achievable," G.M. told us.

"I want to continue to take some of the pressures off my husband financially," said another focus group member. "He is taking care of expenses for his mother, who has been ill for a long time."

Another Boomer, a teacher, told us "I would like to continue to learn about – and pursue – how education impacts kids, and what I can do to affect kids constructively."

"I think retirement would be my next best career move," laughed another panelist, "because I want to do all those things I haven't had time to do for 40 years.

"After that, I would like to write a book to satisfy the urge to tell management what I think of them. After that, I would like to sell it...to make money."

Lifetime motivations

Many of our focus group members – now in the midst of middle-age – offered profound long-term reflections.

One younger Boomer noted: "I'd like to raise my two little miracles to love and respect themselves, and each other.

"And I want to progress in my career to beyond just competence. I went from doing (working in a profession) to teaching it. I have a great opportunity to share a great love with another generation."

"I'd love to play the piano, sail the rest of the way around the world, and save enough to someday be able to retire before I die," said K.H.

Many of our panelists discussed living a healthy life. "I want to continue to practice a level of fitness of mind, body, and spirit," said M.C. "I want to stay young so that I can enjoy good health with our son and his family when that comes along."

"I'd like to live long enough, and be healthy enough, to be actively involved in the lives of my grandchildren," said E.A.

"I'd like to have a nice retirement, including volunteer work, some earnings, and spend more time with my wife," D.J. reflected.

Said one older Boomer: "I'd like to be on the planning committee of our 50th high school reunion, because that means I will live at least another ten years!"

"I'd like to remain self-sufficient as long as possible, to remain unencumbered by material things as much as possible, and to live to play with my grandchildren," said M.F.

Added R.H. "I'd like to have grandchildren, and to live long enough to see my grandchildren. I'd like to spoil my grandchildren...just to get even with my children!"

"I want to be a really good grandmother and be able to teach my grandchildren the values I taught my own girls," said P.M. "The last goal is to try to live a long, happy, healthy life by trying to take care of myself and my husband."

"As one ages," G.M. philosophized, "one should become more Thoreauesque...one chair for personal use, and one chair for company. You don't need a complete living room suite any longer."

"I want to live a life that models respect and concern for our planet, so that those who come after us – our kids and grandkids – have a quality of life that they deserve," said another.

"My three goals," G.L. told us, "are to continue focus on: physical fitness with diet and exercise; mental fitness...never stop reading and learning; and religious fitness...a true long-term investment!"

"I would like to stay as healthy as possible," said L.A., "not give up on life, and grow old with vigor!"

Finally, several people told us they'd like to write a book. Noted one respondent: "Don't all the old saws say 'Write what you know?' In that case, I'd be better off writing about the multitude of indignities that everyday life brings to bear on each of us."

Universal thoughts

A.T. offered insight on planetary matters: "I want to continue being a responsible citizen of the earth, trying to lessen the deleterious effect of my presence here by 'going green' as much as possible.

"My only personal goal is to love and be loved. That's all I can take with me into whatever the future holds."

What did we learn?

1. As we move into our middle years, an orderly and peaceful lifestyle is important to many of us.

2. We expressed an interest in travel. Some would like to visit our nation's historic regions and sports facilities. Others would like to travel internationally, perhaps to visit the regions from which their ancestors came.

3. Financial matters are important to us. We want to be as debt-free as possible. Some of us are financially caring for both our children and our parents.

4. Many of us want to continue learning and growing intellectually. And we would also like to share our knowledge with others.

5. Because of great advances in medical care, we hope for many more healthy years. With those years, we would like to acquire new skills and share more time with our families.

6. Many of us would like to simplify our lifestyles as we age.

7. We want to be responsible citizens of this planet, and to leave it in good condition for generations yet to come.

CHAPTER 24
What have you done that makes you proud?

Just about everybody wants to be appreciated. In our early years, it makes us feel good if a parent or teacher compliments us.

As we get older, we enjoy testing our skills in competitions. Can we run faster, or jump higher, or do math problems quicker?

By the time we move into high school, most of us become aware of both our strengths and weaknesses. If we can match activities we like with those where we excel, we may develop a formula for adult success.

Later on – as we move into our middle years – we still appreciate recognition. But we also enjoy applying our skills, teaching our children or relatives, and passing our knowledge along to others.

What makes you proud? That's the question we put to our focus group.

Self-fulfillment, enlightenment

"I found myself," said one older Boomer, "through the help of much therapy."

"I went back to college and completed my degree," said T.S. "It took me 20 years from start to finish, and I was told by many along the way that it didn't matter, but I'm so glad I did it.

"At the very least, it's an accomplishment of perseverance. It may not have made any difference as to what I did with my life, but it was much harder to learn in my mid-30's, so I give myself credit for going back."

Noted R.R.: "I feel I have lived up to the high standards that were instilled in me by my parents, and that I have done my best never to disgrace my family. I earned a college degree, and I am proud to have been independent all these years, and have never relied on the charity of someone else for a roof over my head.

"I feel I have achieved a comfort level within myself, and that I have proved myself a reliable, loving, and devoted daughter, sister, cousin, aunt, wife, and friend."

"I am proud that I am a trustworthy person," said G.M. "I've just tried to do a good job wherever I've been."

"I renewed my relationship with God," said another.

Parenting, teaching

"I could say raising a wonderful son," said a contemplative K.L. "But we are talking Baby Boomers, and we are supposed to be self-centered. So I guess I would point to getting my pilot's license, sailing halfway around the world in a 70's sailboat, and a successful career."

"I had a part in the creation of two amazing little humans," said T.C. "As a child, and even as a young adult, I thought accomplishment meant something career-related. But every time I look at my two beautiful creations, I know differently."

"I succeeded in marrying a good man, the product of which is a wonderful daughter," said M.F.

"I'm proud that I raised two children without much help," noted S.W.

"I am so proud of my husband and three girls," said P.M. "I was a stay-at-home mom and took part in everything they did, whether I was wanted or not.

"My husband and I made the commitment to be the best parents we could be if we decided to have children. Both of us had good childhoods.

"All three of our girls have college educations, and are all taking care of themselves with successful careers. All have found their husbands – or husbands-to-be – and have started on their own lives."

"I'm proud of having our son," emphasized one older Boomer, "and parenting him in a way that was much better than when I grew up. We gave him many opportunities for a great education, and he has taken advantage of it.

"I cared for my parents as they unraveled in their later years, and our son was able to love them – and experience their love – by our having a close connection with them."

"I am gratified," said another Boomer, "that I spent 30 years in the Air Force helping provide health care worldwide, and that I continue supporting organizations that provide health care to indigents."

Said another contemplative respondent: "I've worked really hard to be a good husband, physician, business person, community volunteer, and friend."

Finally, we loved this statement from A.T., which gets right to the essence of accomplishment: "Simply put, I've been a good person. I've striven to walk gentle upon the earth, to leave everything and everyone better off than they were before I got there. And to show for my efforts, I am loved. That's all that really matters, isn't it?"

What did we learn?

1. Knowing more about oneself helps us to better understand others.

2. Defining goals and then accomplishing them builds self-esteem.

3. A college degree was a major goal of many Boomers, which may explain why we've had more formal education than other generations.

4. Trustworthiness, reliability, and spirituality are major concerns of this generation.

5. Many of us view parenting as our highest calling.

6. For the most part, we have been eager to take advantage of educational opportunities, and we want our children to do the same.

7. As we've moved into mid-life, we've tried to pass our skills and knowledge along to others.

8. The Information Age has made us aware of world issues like hunger and disease, and many of us try to help alleviate these problems.

CHAPTER 25
Ten school lessons we never forgot

Virtually all of us went to school in the dark ages, B.C. (before computer). But lessons learned back then still stick to us like rubber cement.

Mostly we learned this stuff on the playground, in the lunchroom, or at events like football games or dances.

Here are discoveries I personally stumbled upon. What did you learn?

1. Bells rule our life. The last high school bell, for instance, alerts us that we need to prepare for a career. Every year when the birthday bell rings, we're reminded that time moves faster than a cheetah on a treadmill.

2. Don't eat off your friend's plate until he tells you it's OK. It's better to leave the lunchroom a little hungry than a little bruised.

3. Getting picked first on someone's team means that the person recognizes your skill. Getting picked last means you should explore some of your other gifts.

4. Everyone can contribute. The tallest guy may be your basketball star. The smartest girl might be the school's spelling champion. (My special gift: Teachers could point to me as a bad example.)

5. Never throw food. That's true in the elementary lunchroom, at the senior prom, and for nearly all weddings.

6. Hold your tongue. (Not literally, of course, because it gets drool on your hand.) We learn quickly that if we make a silly or unkind statement, we can't take it back.

7. You win a few, you lose a few, and you get disqualified if you forget to show up. Therefore, an alarm clock makes a great graduation gift.

8. Teachers are some of the greatest people you'll ever know.

9. Everybody needs a coach. Find older people whose skills you admire, and ask how they acquired them.

10. Life is not high school. Move on. (That's a good thing, because if life were a geometry class I'd never figure out the angles.)

CHAPTER 26
What the heck happened to Main Street?

When you get a few moments, close your eyes and try to picture what your downtown's Main Street looked like 30 or 40 years ago. Now, I'm not psychic, but I suspect your street looked much like a mythical town I'll talk about now.

So let's walk down this Path of the Past, and see what we find:

Here we are at the courthouse. It's been there for ages, right? The brick is fading, but we don't take it for granite. (Ha, ha! "Take it for granite." Get it?)

But once we leave this old building, things have changed big-time. Remember the little hamburger stand across the street? It's gone now, replaced by a national chain fast-food place.

Just to the left in the first block was a great little jewelry store, run by two generations of merchants. It's gone too. The family aged, and folks started spending more time at the malls than on Main.

Our stroll continues

In the next several blocks stood two competing, family-owned department stores. They're gone too. One stayed downtown, eventually closed, and sold the real estate. The other tried strip shopping centers in the 1960's, but found it hard to compete with the mall concept.

A couple blocks further down, three majestic theaters welcomed movie premieres and visiting stars who made personal appearances to boost ticket sales. Those huge auditoriums welcomed thousand of fans over three or four decades, and attracted out-of-town visitors as well.

But those grand auditoriums are gone too.

MEDIA CHANGES SINCE THE MID-1970'S

In the early and middle 1970's, most large cities in the United States had at least two daily newspapers, and some had three. Some papers also offered morning and evening editions.

Today, few major cities have more than one major paper. And that paper probably gets published only once a day, in the morning.

Weekly newspapers have changed, too. Many small-town papers suffered as retail trade declined downtown, and moved to mega-stores between towns, or to shopping malls. On the plus side, there are probably more classified ad and "shopper" papers, many that carry some local stories.

Magazines – I think most would agree that general-interest magazines have declined, replaced by specialty magazines. Trade and industry magazines appear to be more "vertical." That is, a magazine may choose not to focus on an entire industry, but only on a segment of it.

Radio – The two biggest changes in radio this past quarter-century are (1) the emergence of the "talk" (call-in) format and (2) the increase in FM radio stations.

Few would dispute that radio is primarily an "in-vehicle" medium, or that it completely dominates any medium when people get into their cars.

Television – Huge changes here! Many more stations, mostly on cable or satellite. Pay-per-view shows and "infomercials" add another dimension. TV is often called the dominant medium because people spend so much time watching it.

Worldwide Web – Twenty-five – even ten – years ago folks might define the Internet as a basketball league. But today we all know how pervasive it can be, and how much potential it shows.

Strip shopping centers and shopping malls

Away from downtown, things have changed too. The old "strip shopping centers" of the 1960's and 1970's still exist, but their tenants have changed. Gone are many mom-and-pop specialty retailers (bicycle shops, five-and-dime variety stores, hardware stores, independent pharmacies, family hamburger shops, card stores, etc.). National chains – either company-owned or franchise operations – replaced them.

What about enclosed shopping malls? One person described them as the "Main Streets of the 21st century," and who can deny it? Folks gather in these giant weather-controlled environments, snack at the food courts, and wander through mostly mass-merchant stores.

Not long ago, a friend told me that "Driving across the country is different today. Thirty years ago each town had its own personality and architecture. Today, they've all got the same franchise operations, the same motel chains, the same fast food places."

What did we learn?

1. American towns are becoming generic. The good side is that we're familiar with the chains, and know what to expect. The bad side is that we know what to expect, but sometimes we want something different.

2. It's hard to tell our children what sort of world we grew up in. When our parents told us about their early lives, they could quickly point to established stores and institutions. We'd like to do the same thing, but many of the places we remember just aren't around.

3. Change is inevitable. But for the last decade or so, change has become the rule. If we cannot adapt to change, if we cannot embrace it, we will be left behind. If you've thought about updating your resume', going back to school, tackling a new training course, even preparing for a new, modern career...now's the time.

4. After interviewing loads of people, I'm convinced that the driving force in our world is COMMUNICATION. Consumers demand that it must always be faster, clearer, better, and inexpensive. Communications companies and innovators reinvented the world in the 20th century, and they will reinvent it in the 21st.

Chapter 27
Going back, looking forward: Nine tips for a memorable class reunion

A book on Boomer secrets would be incomplete without a short chapter on reconnecting with your contemporaries. One of the best ways is through your high school class reunion. It doesn't matter if you graduated 20, 30, or 40 years ago. You all shared some turbulent, life-changing years.

And reunions can be loads of fun. I know, because I go to them all the time...and many aren't even my class. Heck, I've probably been to as many reunions as a name badge salesman.

The key to successful reunions, folks tell me, is "building a community." That is, every person invited needs to feel that he/she was part of a special group. But how do you do that?

1. Begin locally – Those still living in the same town as your high school form the primary reunion committee. If you live close to your school, how many of your fellow grads still live within your zip code?

2. Initial gathering – Call the local folks you know first, then ask them to call classmates they know. Schedule an informal lunch or dinner at an inexpensive, easy-to-find local restaurant.

3. Include everybody – The larger the planning committee the better! At the initial event, ask each person to bring either – or both – mailing and e-mailing addresses for all classmates with whom they're still in contact.

4. Class archivist – Appoint one member – preferably one with solid computer skills – to develop a database or spreadsheet that lists important details of each class member (name, address, city/state/zip, home phone, business phone, cell phone, fax, and…most important, e-mail!

5. Set a date – Preferably about a year away. Then, send that date – and location, if possible – to local newspapers, radio stations, and your old high school.

6. Ask for donations – This is really hard to do, but it's tough to grow a reunion without seed money. Those early dollars can help you (a) buy postage, (b) fund a classmate to set up a solid e-mail database, (c) book a location, and (d) fund long distance phone charges to call folks who are out of town,

7. Build that database – An old school phone directory is a good place to start. Call parents, brothers, and sisters of classmates. Talk to people who graduated the years before and after you.

8. E-mail – The best way we found to gather both new addresses and information is by sending <u>frequent</u> e-mails to classmates. Another idea: Create an "Each one, reach one" campaign by asking every classmate on your current database to find at least one other class member.

9. Request a reply – In each of your e-mailings to those already on your database, give them a reason to reply. Those reasons could be to (a) send a donation, (b) fill out a questionnaire, or (c) take part in a classmate survey. Said one of our classmates: "The more we mailed to them, the more interested they seemed to become."

10. This is critical: If a person expresses interest, give him/her a job that gets that individual involved! (Even out-of-towners might call classmates within their regions, or send out a few information letters.) People who get involved may feel a renewed sense of belonging, and will want the reunion to succeed.

Chapter 28
The final chapter: Should you write your own obituary?

According to a recent issue of The Mouser Report (a business newsletter), Boomers are paying more attention to obituaries these days. There are even some obituary web sites, like www.obitpage.com and www.obituaryforum.blogspot.com.

Why? Maybe because the older we get, the more we focus on mortality.

So let's think about it: when you kick the bucket in 2050, or 2070, or whatever…should you let somebody else – possibly not even a Boomer – write your obituary? Certainly not!

For the sake of your spouse, children, and grandkids – and for the obituary sites that'll run it – you should tell future generations about your thoughts, accomplishments, and farsightedness…even if you're too dead to need glasses anymore.

Just in case you thought this little book wasn't worth what you paid for it, here's another "value-added" benefit. Use the "sample obituary template" below to simplify your own final tribute.

Then, store it away in some safe place…like next to your will, or near some of those valuable old rockers' reunion concert tickets.

+ + + + + + + + + + + + + +

Babe E. Boomer, age 130,
dies during 100 meter dash

(Note: This is not your real name, age, or cause of demise. But it makes a good headline.)

Babe E. Boomer passed away last week during an Ultra-Senior Track and Field Competition. Onlookers say he crossed the finish line just before he finished permanently.

Boomer – a child of the mid-1950's – lived a remarkable, accomplished life. Born in the middle of the 20th century, he endured food chemical additives, beltless car seats, record players, and even a gas shortage during 13 decades. "When you think about it," commented a track meet official, "he ran out of gas here, too."

Boomer attended more schools than a class ring salesman, and earned so many degrees he ran out of wall space. The day after his untimely death, he was scheduled to begin classes for another degree because – in his own words -- "It's time to think about a mid-life career change."

Like many contemporaries, Boomer did not believe in aging. He had his face lifted so much he began to breathe through his navel. After his seventh knee replacement, he gave up high jumping.

Also like many others his age, Boomer spoke via a pre-recorded video at his own funeral. "Dad didn't want some stranger to give his eulogy," said Boomer's son Babe, Jr. "Also, he wanted to say a lot of nice things about himself."

Boomer's service lasted over three hours, punctuated by musical selections from his many decades on earth. "We felt attendees would be comfortable with a combination of old time rock-and-roll and soothing elevator music," his son added.

His rambling eulogy offered comments about family and friends. But the highlight came when he discussed what it meant to be a Baby Boomer.

"Kids don't realize how easy they have it these days," he groused. "In my youth we drank water from the garden hose, and thought it tasted fine. We didn't text message in class. We just wrote notes with a # 2 pencil, and passed them to each other.

"And back then, we weren't afraid of fatty food. We thought triglycerides were space aliens."

Boomer had no graveside services. Instead, he left instructions that his body be frozen immediately after death, and thawed out if – at some later date – it became possible to bring him back.

Survivors include his wife, 2.3 children (the statistically average number for a Baby Boomer), 17 grandchildren, too many great-grandchildren to count, an antique mid-1960's convertible with dual exhausts, and a variable rate mortgage he refinanced 11 times.

+ + + + + + + + + + + + + + +

But seriously, friends…how we deal with the next 20 or 30 years – or, if we're lucky, more years than that – can profoundly affect the lives of future generations.

What can you and I do tomorrow, next week, and next year to contribute to a better planet? We've got the age and the experience to make a difference.

When it comes to your final ceremony, what will friends and loved ones say about you?

CHAPTER 29
Epilogue

So how do we sum up this book of quotes and tips from folks born between 1946 and 1964? We know that if you're over 25, you've already received hundreds of suggestions from parents, teachers, and friends. How many of these do you still recall?

Frankly, after over five decades on earth, this Boomer particularly remembers ten lessons that really helped. Here they are:

1. Prepare for the future, but take time to savor the present moment.

2. The video of life doesn't have a "rewind" button. You can't correct yesterday. You can only try to do better today and tomorrow.

3. Treat your parents well. Without them, you wouldn't be here.

4. The four greatest gifts you can give your children are love, acceptance, encouragement, and preparation. The road of life can sometimes be an uphill climb.

5. Try to learn something new every day, and try to teach something every day.

6. An open mind welcomes both sunlight and rain. Listen carefully to new ideas, and to people with whom you disagree. Every person you meet therefore becomes your teacher.

7. Life is a cooperative venture. Those who lived before us left us some wonderful instruction manuals. We call them "history books."

8. Inspire others to read and write better. These are two of life's most important skills.

9. Nearly everybody you meet is dealing with some sort of problem. Be kind and forgiving.

10. Choose a career that fits your personality, and life goals that help others.

CHAPTER 30
Bonus: 26 startling predictions for Boomers and their children

You've probably guessed we couldn't end the book without making some outrageous predictions. I mean, 187 ideas from our contemporaries require more than just a meager listing.

So here's what we think will happen to Boomers – and the many, many lives they influence – in the next few years:

1. Social Security – The system will experience a tremendous jolt as about <u>4 million Boomers per year</u> quality for benefits from 2008-2026. Our guess: Boomers will be encouraged to work longer, and offered incentives to apply for Social Security at a later age... perhaps 70 or more.

2. Part-time work – As many healthy Boomers retire from full-time employment, they will seek part-time work. Hundreds of new jobs will be created specifically for individuals who want to (a) work at home, (b) do that work by computer or phone, and (c) need to work to supplement retirement benefits.

3. More college – A surprising number of Boomers will enroll in college undergraduate or graduate programs. This will create a demand for more teachers and more degree opportunities.

4. Sports frenzy – Here's an amazing, positive thing about loads of Boomers...they don't want to quit exercising! With young adults adopting a healthy lifestyle, and aging Boomers still embracing it, look for more exercise inventions and more retailers supplying them.

5. Replacement parts – We're talkin' body parts. How many of us know family members who've had knees or hips replaced? We suspect Boomers will create a growing market in human tissue repair/replacement. What body part will be developed next? We don't want to think about it.

6. Gender power – Boomer women and their daughters, voting in increasingly greater numbers, will determine Presidential and Congressional election winners for the next 20–30 years.

7. Dressing up – Boomers who defined relaxed clothing trends and "casual Friday" at work will once again embrace the suit, tie, polished shoes, and the elegant look.

8. Urban dwellers – Children of the 1950's and 1960's whose parents purchased suburban homes will move into elegant condos in the city as they become empty nesters.

9. Shrinkage – Boomers who once sought larger suburban homes – and still want to live outside the city – will soon seek smaller, ultra-modern, efficient autonomous dwellings, which have little exterior property to maintain.

10. Two generation homes – Here's another possibility: many Boomers' children may decide – after high school and college – to return to live with

their parents. New credit restrictions may also make it harder for young adults to qualify for loans. This situation could trigger a demand for low-cost, low-square-footage, high-efficiency homes.

11. Retirement communities – The Boomer generation will suggest new amenities like workout facilities, athletic competitions, health food dining spots, and computer-friendly homes and public areas.

12. Visual communication – Because we Boomers grew up with TV, we'll likely want future electronic communications to be visual too. Look for more video phones and high-quality computer cameras.

13. More reality shows – This Boomer is convinced reality shows are only beginning. Today we see dance, singing, cooking, and design competitions. And, of course we've got celebrity reality shows. What's next? How about animal IQ contests?

14. Voluminous video – High-tech video cameras, great computer video editing programs, and innovative amateur videographers will combine to produce outstanding short segments suitable for airing on multiple computer video sites. Online videos will compete with TV for prime-time viewers.

15. Radio? – Radio will continue to grow in many forms, providing people who have different interests a medium where they can voice concerns. Think of radio as a "town forum" for many, many new demographic segments.

16. Interactive television – Shopping and call-in programs are very popular today. We predict new opportunities to react to television shows. Wouldn't it

be fun to watch a televised drama, then vote on how you wanted it to end?

17. Back to public school – We foresee a revival of the American public school. This educational system, which served our generation so well, has been threatened in recent years as parents sought private, charter, or home-schooling alternatives.

We will once again discover what our grandparents and parents discovered long ago: <u>every American will benefit from training in classical English, history, math, and science basics and interaction with all socioeconomic levels. The quality of our society depends on a literate population.</u>

18. Communication courses – Technology and online career opportunities will create new jobs that require the ability to write well. We hope for new emphasis in English, school newspaper, yearbook, literary magazine, speech, drama, and debate courses.

19. Condensed messages – 21st century society requires condensed information. Look for new, shortened versions of books, instruction manuals, and news delivery.

20. Destination events – Today "destination weddings" are increasingly popular. The engaged couple, family and friends often journey to a distant location for a theme wedding.

We think a slightly different scenario will be made available to Boomers. For instance, wouldn't it be fun to take a tour of "major historical sites of the 1960's/1970's?"

21. Grandchildren – Because our generation's placed a high emphasis on education, we also emphasized that

for our children, too. Our guess is there will soon be financial and educational products offered to support the education/training goals of present and future grandchildren.

22. Volunteerism – We think large numbers of Boomers will begin to volunteer at schools, adult care centers, hospitals, and charitable organizations as they move into late middle age.

Our focus group expressed a desire to help those less fortunate. This has been reinforced by other studies and statistical information.

23. Individually-tailored careers – In the next 20 years, several new one-person corporations will enter the workplace. We will see individuals who make a living doing very specialized work for tiny market segments of major industries. The "age of the specialist" will continue to grow.

24. Revitalized downtowns – You're already seeing many cities rebuilding their downtown areas into large shopping, dining, and entertainment facilities.

25. Funeral alternatives – Our generation has created several alternative lifestyles, so it's no surprise if we do the same thing when we quit breathing. We speculate more people will stage novel, offbeat funerals, cremations, organ donations, and even deep-freezing.

26. Our history – In the next 30 years, several historians will attempt to analyze and define us.

We wish them luck.